Success with
TRUSTS

Success with
TRUSTS

How trusts protect
your assets

ROSS HOLMES
LLB (HONS)

REED

Acknowledgments

I wish to express my thanks to the team at Ross Holmes Limited for their assistance with this book, Malcolm Lake for writing the foreword, and the publishers, Reed Publishing (NZ) Ltd, for their invaluable assistance in producing a quality book.

Published by Reed Books, a division of Reed Publishing (NZ) Ltd, 39 Rawene Rd, Birkenhead, Auckland, New Zealand. Associated companies, branches and representatives throughout the world.

Established in 1907, Reed Publishing (NZ) Ltd is New Zealand's largest book publisher, with over 300 titles in print.

For details on all these books visit our website:
www.reed.co.nz

© 2000 Pacific Trusts
The author asserts his moral rights in the work.

ISBN 0 790 00772 X
First published 2000

Edited by Carolyn Lagahetau
Designed by Graeme Leather

Printed in New Zealand

This book is dedicated to my wife Janet,
who makes my life complete.
Without her assistance it would not have been possible.

It is also dedicated to my children
Tonya, Michael, Christopher, Katherine,
Jasmine, Robert, Andrew and Jolene.

The need to provide for the future prosperity of my family
has been the principal motivation behind the development
of my asset protection practice.
As a result, I have for many years practised what I preach —
personal poverty and a rich trust.
It works.

C ONTENTS

9. SUCCESS THROUGH USING AN EXPERT TO PREPARE YOUR ASSET PROTECTION PLAN

10. WHAT IS A TRUST?

11. SUCCESS THROUGH MAKING SURE YOUR ASSET PROTECTION PLAN WORKS

16. SUCCESS WITH PROPERTY AND REALTY

F O R E W O R D

If you fail to plan, you plan to fail

ROSS HOLMES

None of us wish to fail. We all want to succeed and achieve our important objectives. We can do this by planning. Trusts should not be scary. Preparing a trust is just like preparing a will; in fact, a trust is similar to a living will — it works while you are alive.

For centuries the wealthy have used trusts to protect their wealth. However, many of us incorrectly believe that trusts are only needed by the rich. We all need to follow the example of the rich and form trusts to succeed. If a trust is established and administered genuinely, as part of your comprehensive asset protection plan, it will help you to achieve your objectives and prosper. It is no secret that many of the wealthy achieve their wealth in this manner.

Ross Holmes points out two simple facts at his Success with Trusts seminars. Firstly, your will cannot protect your assets — it does not work until you die. By then, you have lost what the risks of life are going to take from you. Secondly, personal ownership of assets cannot protect your assets against the risks of life. Such ownership gives you no protection. By personally owning assets you are in essence crossing your fingers and hoping that those risks will not happen to you.

I attended university and graduated with a law degree. Before I met Ross I had been successful in my career as a lawyer and had established my own law firm. Like many lawyers, I had not questioned the 'old ways' of investment, asset ownership or preparing wills. My views changed after attending one of Ross' Success with Trusts seminars. One of the reasons I changed my views is that Ross has proved through his own actions that what he advises others to do works in the real world. Ross is a self-made man, who personally owns very little. The trusts that he has established, however, are worth millions. Ross has substantial business experience and is a director of a number of private companies.

Much of what Ross says challenges the very core of accepted wisdom. Initially, his ideas seemed radical and far-fetched. Then I realised that they were simple common sense. In today's complicated society, it is sometimes difficult to spot the obvious.

I had to put aside my legal training and open my mind in order to accept Ross' views. I am glad that I did. As a result, I am now planning to succeed. I was so convinced by his views that I have also become a member of Ross' team. By removing future risks as much as possible, I have now maximised my chances of success.

I heartily recommend this book to you. It will show you how you can maximise your chances of success. I urge you to accept the challenge and to succeed. The choice is yours.

Malcolm Lake, LLB,
Principal, Malcolm Lake Solicitors,
Rotorua, New Zealand

INTRODUCTION

We are a user-pays society. With an aging population there is increasing pressure on governments to raise more taxes, both during your lifetime and on your death, and to means test government assistance for retirement pensions, health care and long term geriatric care. If that is not bad enough, during your life business failures, law suits, failing to take advantage of the remaining legal tax concessions, new relationship failures, accidents and illness may take your savings from you. On your death, your will may be contested. If any of these misfortunes occur, how can you succeed if you have not planned in advance to avoid such risks? You need not take these risks — with simple planning they can all be minimised or avoided.

The need for planning in advance has long been known to the rich. Through advance planning they avoid such problems. In fact, many of the so-called rich should not be on the rich lists at all. They structure their affairs from day one in order that all-important assets are owned by trusts. Many are relatively poor, but have rich trusts. For example, it was recently reported that one of the Virgin companies run by British entrepreneur Richard Branson had to ask the trustees of Channel Islands-based trusts, which he had established, for financial assistance.

Many of us put off our planning for the wrong reasons. We do not want to face the fact that the worst could happen to us. The reason many of us fail to plan is that we are conditioned to put the possibility of the worst happening to us into the too hard basket — something to be dealt with later, but in reality to be forgotten about if at all possible. We become older and in many cases accumulate more assets. As a consequence, such delays lessen the opportunities for ensuring that our important financial objectives are achieved, and increase the risk of occurrences that could prevent us from achieving those objectives.

This book is designed to help you achieve your important personal and financial objectives through planning. By planning you can achieve financial safety and protection, both during your lifetime and for those you wish to pass your wealth to.

Ross Holmes

1

THE RICH ACHIEVE THEIR OBJECTIVES BY PLANNING

When it comes to the future, there are three kinds of people: those who make it happen, those who let it happen, and those who wonder what happened.

JOHN M. RICHARDSON JR

WHY MANY WHO ARE NOT FROM RICH FAMILIES WILL NOT BECOME WEALTHY

Many of us who are not from wealthy families will never become wealthy. We will continue to do what our parents did, getting the best possible qualifications and getting a good job working for someone else. We feel comfortable and safe following the old ways, and never think to question them. Are they in fact safe? Can they help you to achieve your important objectives?

In their excellent book *Rich Dad, Poor Dad*, Robert Kiyosaki and Sharon Lechter point out that working hard, having children, buying a bigger house, getting paid more (and as a result being taxed more), saving for your children's future education, and saving for retirement, results in

> *that happy couple . . . now trapped in the Rat Race for the rest of their working days. They work for the owners of their company, for the government paying taxes, and for the bank paying off a mortgage and credit cards. If one of your objectives is to become wealthy, it is simply not possible to achieve that objective in the way that the happy couple is trying to. Moreover, your children are likely to follow your example —* 'the happy couple are in turn likely to train their children to do the same.

Self-employment on its own cannot help you achieve great wealth. Many who become self-employed earn their income by charging for their time. You can never become extremely wealthy doing this as there are only so many hours in the day and so much an hour that you can charge.

WHY SOME OF THOSE NOT FROM RICH FAMILIES LOSE THEIR ASSETS

We are brought up to believe that it is safe to do what our parents did: buy assets in our own names and prepare wills leaving assets to our loved ones. However, it is not as safe as it sounds. Consider the following contrasting examples (names have been changed for anonymity).

How to lose your assets

Joe and Mary were New Zealand residents in their seventies. They had done the same as most normal couples. They had worked for employers all their lives, and through their efforts, they owned a house worth $200,000 and had other investments worth $100,000. The income from their investments was used to supplement their government pension. Mary told me that, 'Joe had a stroke when he was 75. As a result of his medical condition after that stroke, it was necessary for him to go into long-term geriatric care. I could not provide the care he needed in our home.' She went on to tell me that she had to spend $55,000 of their investments on Joe's long-term geriatric costs before he qualified for government assistance. 'My own government pension was cut to the single rate, and most of Joe's government pension was taken to meet the costs of his care. I visit Joe every day in his aged care facility. This has greatly increased my car running costs.' As a result, she found it very difficult to live on her pension and her reduced income from investments. 'I cannot sell the house to increase my income as the government would then require all of the sale price to be used for Joe's care. I am so depressed, and feel so helpless.'

Mary's story serves as an example of the problems that a failure to plan can cause.

How to protect your assets

By way of contrast, John and Elizabeth had seen me in 1990, when they were in their early fifties, to set up an asset protection plan. They had a house worth $200,000 and $250,000 worth of investments.

John and Elizabeth told me: 'We want to ensure that the assets are able to be enjoyed by us during our lifetime, and that our two children inherit the assets equally after our death.' They were concerned that if they did nothing the costs of long-term geriatric care might eat up their assets. They formed a trust as part of their asset protection plan and they were appointed as the trustees of the trust (which is the same as being the trustees of a will). They sold the house and investments to the trust at their then current market value, in exchange for Deeds of Acknowledgment of Debt (IOUs) in their favour (that is, they one hundred percent vendor-financed the sale). As they lived in New Zealand[1] (and could only gift $27,000 each per year without gift duty), they gifted the loans to the trust over a period of nine years (gifts are documents saying 'don't pay me back'). They are thrilled with the results. 'Now the trust owes us nothing, and it absolutely owns the house and investments. We still live in the house and pay all the house expenses just as before. We have achieved our objectives one hundred percent.'

If the disaster that happened to Joe and Mary happens to John and Elizabeth in their mid-seventies, the house and investments are likely to be safe. What these stories illustrate is that in today's society if you fail to plan, it is far more difficult, and sometimes not possible, to avoid the risks which could take your assets from you.

Most people blame the government and others for the results of their failure to plan. Blaming others is not going to solve the problem or bring back assets that have been lost. Planning to avoid problems in advance is a far easier and more successful approach.

WHY ARE PEOPLE FAILING TO PROTECT THEIR ASSETS?

The main reason people fail to protect their assets is that many of the lawyers on whom people rely see nothing wrong with wills leaving assets to loved ones personally, or with individual ownership of assets. It is difficult to understand why this is the case.

A will cannot protect your assets. It does not work until you die (often in your late seventies or early eighties). By then you have lost what the risks of life are going to take from you (see chapter 2; these include claims by future partners, law suits, business failures, paying too much tax, incapacity, user-pays charges and taxation on death). The end result of not being aware of the risks which normal wills and individual ownership of assets cause is a loss of control over what happens if such risks occur. Events are then beyond control. This is tragic because it is easy to plan to avoid such risks.

This is why you need to plan (as the rich do) to avoid these risks by having a will that leaves your assets to a trust, and by transferring ownership of your important investments to a trust.

No one has a crystal ball, and the future is bound to bring changes and challenges which we have not previously faced. Anticipating problems and planning to avoid them always works. Planning as problems occur, or as a knee-jerk reaction to witnessing someone else's misfortune, does not work.

How you can improve your chances of acquiring wealth

You can improve your chances of acquiring wealth through education, positive thinking and positive action. My own experience is a case in point.

At age 50, many at my age start thinking about retirement. I am not. Until my mid-forties, I had worked hard as a lawyer selling my time to clients. I had protected my family's assets using trusts, I had a good income, and the trusts I had established had accumulated reasonable assets. However, I could never become very wealthy as there are only so many hours in a week, and only so much that one can charge per hour. I had the academic qualifications needed to become wealthy, and the skills needed to succeed in doing so, but in acting in the normal manner lawyers do (selling time), I was not using my skills to succeed.

At age 45, I changed that virtually overnight through positive thinking and positive action. I have now reduced the time that I spend helping clients to protect their assets, and have employed a team of experts to assist them. I still assist some clients because I enjoy doing so, and I spend the balance of my time managing my business, training my team to ensure that they continue to produce high quality results, and giving seminars. Most importantly, however, I spend time actively looking for and managing worthwhile business and investment opportunities. The trusts that I have established now own interests in rental properties, public and private companies and a property development company. In 1998, allied with a friend's trusts, the combined trusts established a geriatric health care management business. Projects in progress include an international internet 'success' portal and the expansion of my asset protection business.

> The trusts which I established have made many times more money in the past five years than I had made in the previous 22 years of hard work. And this is just the beginning.

HOW THE RICH SUCCEED

For centuries trusts have helped many rich families to keep their wealth. Today's self-made billionaires have achieved their wealth through positive planning and positive action. Many of them have also stayed wealthy through asset protection planning, which has included the use of trusts. In doing so they have taken control of their future. The techniques they use work just as well for those who are not as wealthy.

The growth in the number of millionaires in recent generations shows how well planning works, and that by adopting brave new entrepreneurial ideas it is possible for you to achieve goals in more effective ways than you do now. Multimillionairedom is more widespread than ever before. Of the Forbes 400[2] listing of millionaires in 1999, 251 were entirely self-made.

In his book *How to be a Billionaire*,[3] Martin Fridson, managing director of Merrill Lynch, carried out a comparative study of self-made billionaires. As one of Wall Street's top analysts, Fridson already knew many of those he has written about. He points out that becoming a billionaire is not easy, but there are some common characteristics shared by these wealthy people. They include an ability to recognise personal and analytical strengths and weaknesses in competitors and oneself, a motivation to make money (with that motivation normally being determined by family background), and a preparedness to accept high levels of risk. In addition, one must be able to dominate and out-manage competitors. Not many people have the skills needed to become billionaires.

It is easier to become a millionaire, even if you are not from a wealthy family. The number of millionaires is growing at a rapid pace. In 1989 the number of millionaires had reached 1.3 million in the USA. According to *Forbes* magazine, by 1999 'the number of American families whose net worth is at least $1 million has soared to five million. And demographers predict that over the next ten years the number will quadruple, to 20 million.'

One of the features of this recent increase in wealth is the rising number of self-made young people between the ages of 20 and 35 (especially in fields such as telecommunications and financial services). This contrasts with a generation ago when the rich were mainly white, male and elderly.

A few of the main reasons that others have not used the planning techniques of the rich are:

※ a lack of information about their planning techniques and trusts,

※ some widely held myths about trusts including the incorrect belief that you lose control of your assets by transferring them to a trust, and that establishing a trust is far too difficult,

※ the incorrect belief that only the rich can afford trusts,

※ our in-built belief that nothing is going to go wrong — it only happens to others.

SOME EXAMPLES OF SUCCESS

Warren Buffett, CEO of Berkshire Hathaway,[4] is a self-made billionaire. He is ranked number 3 on the *Forbes* 400 Richest People in America List, and has been on that list since 1982. At age 68, he is estimated by *Forbes* to have a net worth of US$36 billion.

He was able to reach this position by challenging conventional investment wisdom, and making long-term investments in quality companies with leading brand name products that have no serious competition. He has made more money from sharemarket investments than any other person.

'We're more comfortable in that kind of business. It means we miss a lot of very big winners. But we wouldn't know how to pick them out anyway. It also means we have very few big losers — and that's quite helpful over time. We're perfectly willing to trade away a big payoff for a certain payoff.' (Warren Buffett, Berkshire Hathaway Annual Meeting, 1999.)

Buffett's long-term investing philosophy has made plenty of people rich — US$10,000 invested in Berkshire Hathaway in 1965 is now worth US$51 million. But even he can suffer losses. In 1999 large holdings in Coca-Cola, Gillette and Walt Disney led to a substantial drop in the value of Berkshire stock. However, Buffett's investment record remains brilliant; in 33 years Berkshire Hathaway has under-performed the Standard and Poors 500 index only five times.

Paul Allen,[5] who formed Microsoft with Bill Gates, has an estimated worth of US$30 billion. Allen was head of research and new product development, the company's senior technology post. He championed and helped engineer many of the company's most successful products, including MS-DOS®, Word, Windows® and the Microsoft Mouse. He left the company in 1983 after a serious illness and now pursues his vision through a host of independent companies.

Perhaps one of the world's most flamboyant billionaires is **Richard Branson**,[6] the entrepreneur running the Virgin Group. The trusts that he formed in the Channel Islands are estimated to own assets worth US$1.7 billion. Most of his companies are private and domiciled in tax havens such as the Channel Islands. If he had followed in his parents' footsteps he would not have become wealthy. Born in 1950 to an English barrister and his airline hostess wife, Branson did not succeed at school and he skipped college. He has since built an empire of some 200 companies with combined yearly revenues estimated at US$4 billion. His group spans three continents and includes an airline, railway investments, financial services, music stores, cinemas, and cola manufacturing. Branson's risk tolerance levels are higher than those of many billionaires and he has suffered some spectacular failures, with some of his businesses running at a loss. An energetic self-promoter, he was quoted in *Business Week* as saying, 'I want Virgin to be as well-known around the world as Coca-Cola.'

What these self-starters have shown is that we can all take control of our future through education, exploring bold new ideas, positive action and positive planning through business planning, investment planning, and asset protection and trust planning.[7] Certainly some of us will do it better than others, but we can all learn how to plan much better than we do now.

SUMMARY

✦ We all have two fundamental choices: to be smart, plan as the rich do and plan to take the risks out of the future; or do what others do — continue to feel safe and comfortable with 'the old ways' — in reality, crossing our fingers and planning to fail if the worst happens to us.

✦ As a matter of common sense (not law), personal ownership of assets cannot protect your assets against the risks of life.

✦ The major defect of a will is that it cannot protect your assets. It does not work until you die (usually in your late seventies to mid-eighties). By then, you have lost what the risks of life are going to take from you.

2

SUCCESS THROUGH IDENTIFYING RISKS

*Opportunity does not knock, it presents itself
when you beat down the door.*

KYLE CHANDLER

THE RICH SUCCEED BY IDENTIFYING AND PLANNING TO AVOID RISKS

Prior to World War II, only the rich were hit by high taxes and high estate/inheritance taxes. They planned to avoid estate duty/ inheritance taxes by using trusts. They used the income-splitting potential of trusts to legally minimise income tax. They also identified and planned to avoid other risks that could prevent them achieving their important objectives. Very few of the non-rich have followed their example. The major reasons are, firstly, lack of information and secondly, an almost unshakable belief that there is no need to plan as 'the worst is not going to happen to me'.

THE REALITY OF USER-PAYS

The reality is that we now have, and in future will always have, a user-pays society. In western countries governments have introduced user-pays policies in recent generations. These user-pays policies were not foreseen by our parents or our grandparents, and as a result, they could not plan to avoid the often unfair and devastating consequences of these policies.

The pressures to impose user-pays charges will grow. The proportion of the population over 65 is increasing in all western countries. In New Zealand, as at March 1996, the proportion of the population over 65 was 12 percent. It is estimated that by 2031 this proportion will increase to 21 percent.[1]

Additionally, the ratio of working to retired people is dropping, putting increasing pressure on government resources as the needs of the elderly increase. In New Zealand, former Prime Minister Jim

Bolger had referred to New Zealand Treasury estimates that by the year 2040 the ratio of workers to retired would have dropped from the current level of 5:1 to 2:1. He was also reported as stating that, 'It must be clear that a shift of that magnitude will result in fiscal pressures . . . in terms of retirement income and health expenditure.'[2] This trend will increase the pressure on governments to impose even more taxes to meet the resulting costs of caring for the elderly.

RISKS TO AVOID

What are the risks that could prevent us from achieving our important objectives? We have all seen or heard of disaster stories brought about by a failure to plan. The following risks can wreak havoc on your long-term objectives:

- Claims by future partners
- Law suits (being taken to court)
- Failure to plan investments properly
- Failure to plan in business
- Failure to plan for your business succession
- Paying too much tax
- Incapacity
- user-pays charges
- Taxation on death.

SUCCESS THROUGH AVOIDANCE OF CLAIMS BY FUTURE PARTNERS

In 1990 Marjorie was widowed at age 72, after 45 years of marriage. The possibility of marrying again never entered her head. In 1992 she met Richard. She married Richard in 1994 and, letting her emotions get the better of her good sense, she did not enter into a pre-marital agreement. Richard moved into her home, then worth $350,000. I asked her why she had not entered into a pre-marital agreement. 'Richard seemed to be such a gentleman. He treated me so well before our marriage. This marriage was going to be forever. It was not until he moved into my home that I realised he was an alcoholic. His major mood swings caused arguments between us.' In 1998 Richard left Marjorie after four years of marriage. Because there was no pre-marital agreement Richard was entitled to half the value of the house. Marjorie concluded, 'It was just so unfair. As my only other asset was a term deposit of $100,000, and my only income was my government pension and a small amount of interest income, I could not afford to pay him half of the value of the home at the time of our separation.' As the house had then increased in value to $400,000, Marjorie was required to pay Richard $200,000. To do so she had to sell the house and buy another valued at half that value. The result was a disaster. She pointed out that, 'I wanted my three children to inherit everything after I died. Now their inheritance has almost been halved, and I have lost the home which my first husband and I had lived in for over 30 years.'

By way of contrast, Del, a long-term client, had formed a trust after the death of her husband.

Del too had been married for over 40 years, when she was widowed in her early seventies. She had attended one of my seminars, and realised that by forming a trust as part of an asset protection plan she could take the risks out of the future. This would allow her to provide for her own needs, and to ensure that her two children inherited what was left over following her death. She sold her home and term investments to the trust. She met Paul three years after her first husband died and married him a year later. Before getting married she sought my advice and entered into a pre-marital agreement. That agreement provided that the trust's home and term investments were to remain as assets belonging to the trust under all circumstances. As it turned out, 'My marriage is extremely happy. However, if Paul or I have to go into long-term geriatric care, the home and term investments have been protected as far as is possible. I feel at ease knowing that my children's inheritance is safe.'

You will succeed by planning in advance to protect your important investments. Failing to plan places them at risk. Property claims can be made by new partners for those with and without present partners. None of us can say that we will never remarry, no matter what our age is. If you marry, or remarry, and in some countries if you live in a *de facto* relationship (in some countries whether with the same sex or the opposite sex), your new partner will usually receive half the value of your house, furniture, car, boat and other assets after a certain period of marriage or *de facto* marriage. This risk can be avoided if you sign a pre-relationship or pre-marital agreement. However, in some countries such agreements can be set aside by a court.

Such problems affect not only you, but also the inheritances that you wish to pass to your loved ones in their own names. You need to seek legal advice that pertains to your circumstances and your country of residence regarding this aspect of asset protection planning.[3]

SUCCESS THROUGH PLANNING TO AVOID PAYING TOO MUCH TAX

In order to succeed it is necessary to take advantage of the few legitimate tax breaks that governments permit us to have. As tax laws vary considerably from country to country, legal advice pertaining to your circumstances and your country must be taken.[4] In a number of countries taxation can be legally reduced by trusts owning income producing assets, and distributing all or part of such income to beneficiaries who are on lower taxation rates. For example, in New Zealand, as from 1 April 2000:

- ❉ Individuals with an income of over $60,000 pay taxation on that portion of the income over $60,000 at a rate of 39 percent.

- ❉ Companies are taxed at 33 percent.

- ❉ Trusts are taxed at 33 percent if the income is not distributed to beneficiaries, and at beneficiary's rates if the income is paid to them. The New Zealand Government has proposed that from 1 April 2001, income of trusts distributed to beneficiaries under 18 will (with some limited exceptions) be taxed at 33 percent.

Accordingly, if you are self-employed and operate a company owned by a trust in New Zealand, it may be possible (depending on your circumstances) to legitimately avoid the 39 percent tax rate.

Success through appointing people to manage your affairs if you are incapacitated

We can all become incapacitated through accident, illness or age. None of us know whether or when such incapacity will occur.

> Peter, a 31-year-old businessperson, suffered permanent brain damage as a result of a work accident. Like many people of his age, he had not seen the need to get his lawyer to prepare an enduring power of attorney that would have appointed his wife Mary to manage his affairs in the event of his becoming incapacitated. As a result, Mary was forced to apply to the court to grant her the power to manage Peter's property affairs. The process cost $7500 in legal fees, medical specialist's fees and the fee for the lawyer appointed by the court to represent Peter. Fortunately, they had just enough savings to pay the fees. If Peter had planned it would have cost less than $100 to get his lawyer to prepare the enduring power of attorney.

> Elizabeth prepared an enduring power of attorney as part of her asset protection plan. When she was affected by dementia at age 75 and lost the ability to manage her financial affairs, her brother and I, as her attorneys, were able to manage her financial affairs without the need for any court application. Her advance planning saved unnecessary costs and delays.

In countries or states that recognise enduring powers of attorney, you can avoid problems by appointing those who you believe are best equipped to look after your property and welfare interests if you are incapacitated. If you do not, then the court will choose who will look after your affairs. Through planning you avoid the need for someone else to decide for you. You also avoid the costs of a court application that will likely be many times more than the costs of your asset protection plan.

SUCCESS THROUGH PLANNING TO AVOID
USER-PAYS CHARGES

In many western countries the government will pay for your long-term geriatric care costs only if you satisfy stringent income and asset testing criteria. One of the reasons I specialise in asset protection planning is that I personally have seen the disasters which a failure to plan can cause.

> My grandparents had worked hard as farmers all their lives. They paid for my mother's university education and her wedding, and they saved for their retirement. They survived the Depression of the 1930s, a major fire that destroyed their home, and a major earthquake. Despite these setbacks, they retired with a reasonable house and modest savings. My grandfather then died, leaving all of his assets to my grandmother. She required long-term geriatric care, which progressively used up most of their life savings. As a result, my mother only received a small inheritance.

The reality is that government means testing of long-term geriatric care frequently results in those with modest assets being stripped of their complete life savings. It is not a just system. What are the odds of it happening to you? In New Zealand, approximately seven percent of the population over 65 are in long-term geriatric care. At age 85, approximately one-third of the population have dementia.

Why do more people not insure against this risk through an asset protection plan? After all, most of us insure our home and its contents against the unlikely event of them burning down or being substantially damaged. Over the years, we pay many thousands of dollars for this essential protection, without questioning the obvious need. The costs of long-term geriatric care can be as devastating as damage to our home and its contents. At least if your house burns down you are left with the land; if you need long-term geriatric care it is likely you may have to dispose of your house to subsidise your care. Don't forget, these risks may affect not only you, but other loved ones such as children and grandchildren. By planning in advance, as you do with house insurance, you can avoid or minimise such risks. Generally, government means testing requires you to have minimal assets before you qualify for any subsidies.[5]

In New Zealand, long-term geriatric care over the age of 65 is income- and asset-tested. The maximum assets you are permitted to have in order to qualify for the government subsidy are as follows.

New Zealand residential care subsidy means test

	Can you keep your home?	Assets you can keep
Single	$15,000	No
Couple — both in a resthome	$30,000	No
Couple — one in a resthome	$45,000	Yes

The government assumes that most people will leave their planning until later in life, when the prospects of long-term geriatric care seem far more real. For that reason, in a number of countries governments decline to pay for long-term geriatric care when those needing that care have disposed of or gifted assets prior to needing such care. In New Zealand, the Social Security Act 1964[6] contains anti-avoidance provisions. These are intended to prevent you from giving away assets and/or income in order to qualify for residential care subsidies. The Act provides:

> *In any case where the Director-General is satisfied that any person —*
> *(a) who has applied for a financial means assessment under this section; or*
> *(b) whose financial means have been assessed under this section*

> *— or that person's spouse, has directly or indirectly deprived himself or herself of any income or realisable assets, the Director-General, in the Director-General's discretion, may calculate or, as the case may be, revise the calculation of the assets and annual income of that person and his or her spouse as if the deprivation had not occurred.*

Despite this broad anti-avoidance measure, as a matter of policy, in New Zealand applicants for residential care subsidies are asked only if they have disposed of any assets in the previous five years. This catches the majority of people out as they have only started planning later in life. Those of us who plan in advance, using a trust as part of an asset protection plan, can often avoid such tragedies.

SUCCESS THROUGH PLANNING TO AVOID TAXATION ON DEATH

In New Zealand, there is currently no estate duty or capital gains tax.[7] Labour is currently carrying out a total review of the New Zealand tax system. The New Zealand Labour Party's 1996 election manifesto promised the reintroduction of estate duty on estates of more than $400,000. Until October 1998, they promised that they would '. . . reinstitute . . . taxing estates . . . to raise an extra $100 m . . . to go towards abolishing asset testing for those . . . in need of geriatric care'.

Labour's coalition partner, the Alliance, has a current policy of introducing death duty on estates of more than $500,000.

In Australia estate duty has been replaced by a capital gains tax that now applies on death. It raises far more income each year than estate duty did for the Australian government in all the years that Australia had estate duty. This is because it applies to everyone without a trust (with minor exceptions).[8]

The amount of estate duty or capital gains tax payable on death is often maximised by loved ones inheriting regardless of their circumstances (whether they will benefit or not), often later in life. This minimises their chances of protecting the inheritance, and maximises what the government and others can take from them.

Advance planning using a trust as part of an asset protection plan can help to avoid or substantially reduce liability for estate duty or capital gains tax on death. Expert assistance is required as this is a highly specialised area of law.

OWNING ASSETS PERSONALLY CANNOT PROTECT THEM AGAINST RISK

If you own assets personally, what protection does that give you against claims by future partners, law suits, business failure, paying too much tax, incapacity, user-pays charges or taxation on death?

Has any advisor told you that personally owning assets is dangerous? Lawyers and accountants usually consider which ownership structure will produce the best taxation benefits (as they must), but do not advise their clients that personally owning assets is dangerous. As a matter of common sense (not law), personal ownership of assets cannot protect your assets against the risks of life. Think about it. How can it possibly give you any protection?

By personally owning assets you are essentially crossing your fingers and hoping that those risks will not happen to you. Worse still, as personally owned assets go up in value, so does your wealth. As your wealth increases, your ability to protect it decreases, as you have less time to gift it in and more of it to gift. If you do not place the assets in a trust from day one, stamp duty, capital gains tax or other taxation liability on sale of the assets to the trust may make it too expensive an option for them to be transferred later.

The end result is that by failing to plan many have lost control over what happens. The risks of life then control what happens. When you die your partner (if you have one) or other loved ones normally inherit all of your wealth, again exposing it to risk. Sooner or later the risks of life will strike and take the assets (or some of them), simply because of a failure to plan.

SUMMARY

→ Each of the risks detailed above can affect you, your partner (if any), your children (or other loved ones), and future generations. If you do not form a trust as part of an asset protection plan, your loved ones are likely to follow your example and not do so either.

→ One of the reasons the rich get richer is that they, their children and succeeding generations plan. One of the reasons that the poor and middle class do not get richer is that they often fail to plan.

→ We can all take control of our future by seeking and exploring bold new ideas, education, positive action and positive planning through careful business, investment and asset protection and trust planning.

→ One of the main reasons many of us fail to protect our assets is that many of the lawyers on whom we rely see nothing wrong with personal ownership of assets. This is tragic, because so many risks are easy to plan to avoid if a trust owns your important investments.

3

SUCCESS THROUGH A TRUST OWNING YOUR IMPORTANT ASSETS

If you own nothing, there is nothing
which anyone can take from you.

ROSS HOLMES

SUCCESS THROUGH YOU SPENDING
AND THE TRUST INVESTING

The object of asset protection planning is personal poverty and a rich trust. This is best achieved by keeping it simple. Too often the simplest solutions are overlooked because they sound too good to be true.

In order to succeed, the trust invests (unless there are taxation or cost reasons which prevent this) and you spend. As the trust invests it gets richer. As you spend you get poorer. If you have nothing, others can take nothing from you — at least if you plan well in advance of problems.

Long-term clients William and Samantha owned a removal company, a substantial home and a number of rental properties. As part of their asset protection plan, they immediately sold all but two of the shares in their company and all their properties to the trusts they had established. William and Samantha are now paid market salaries for their work by the company. These are paid into their personal bank accounts, these accounts being used solely for personal expenditure.

When I recently went over the trust's records with Samantha, she said, 'It was just so simple. We thought it was going to be so hard.' William remained CEO, but Samantha resigned as a director so that she had no liability to others as a director. She said, 'I am glad that I no longer have my neck on the line. Being called general manager sounds just as good.' They have no difficulty running the trusts. 'Instead of dipping into the company's bank account, as we used to every time we needed extra money, I am paying into the trusts' bank account the surplus profits of the company, as the trusts are the major shareholders. We do not need as much money now as the trusts own the properties, pay the bank mortgages and make all investments. All we need in our personal bank accounts is what we personally spend. The trusts are actually saving much better than we were, as the money is never in our personal bank accounts to waste.' Since that time the wealth of the trusts has grown substantially. Through a regular gifting programme, William and Samantha have now achieved personal poverty and rich trusts.

They were so impressed with what they achieved that they have formed trusts for their two daughters to buy what would otherwise have been their daughters' first houses. 'The children will be personally poor their entire lives, and will also end up with a rich trust. Each of our daughters gifts her savings to the trust each year. Their asset protection will succeed one hundred percent. We should have started when we were younger.'

In 1990, Bill and Joy started their trust through their general practitioner family lawyer. They only sold their family home to the trust. 'We were told by our lawyer that as our house was worth $250,000 it was going to take us five years to gift at $27,000 each per year. The lawyer said there was no point selling our company (which was then worth $200,000) to the trust until the first lot of gifting was finished.' That sounded logical to them. They assumed that their lawyer knew what she was doing, even though she was not a specialist. Unfortunately, 'Over the next five years the company's business expanded, and we saved $500,000 from the company's profits. By 1995 the company was worth $500,000 as a result of the increase in its profitability.' As the gifting of the house was completed in 1995, they then sold the company to the trust for $500,000 and in addition sold the investments represented by the savings of $500,000, a total of $1 million. 'We now realise that we should have sold everything to the trust at once. What would have taken us four years to gift at a value of $200,000 will now take us 20 years to gift.' This is sixteen years longer than if everything had been sold to the trust at the same time in 1990. They now regret not having their asset protection plan prepared by an expert.

As Bill and Joy are now aware, you cannot achieve personal poverty and a rich trust if you are getting wealthier as a result of personal savings out of private company or investment income.

There is nothing illegal or wrong with the re-allocation of income. It does not need to involve tax avoidance. Often the same amount of tax is paid in total. Professional taxation advice must always be sought, as taxation laws vary from country to country and frequently change.

By transferring income earning assets to the trust (including private company shares), the trust is then making savings from income, not you. The trust makes the savings and gains the increase in value rather than you personally making the gain.

SUMMARY

→ You cannot achieve your objective of personal poverty and a rich trust if you are making personal capital gains or savings from income on assets you have not sold to your trust. In both cases, you will always be increasing your wealth. This occurs because the overall asset protection programme has not been carefully thought out (often because it was not prepared by a specialist).

4

A WILL LEAVING IMPORTANT ASSETS TO OTHERS CANNOT PROTECT YOUR ASSETS

*Life is short, and the time we waste
in yawning never can be regained.*

STENDHAL

A WILL DOES NOT PROTECT IMPORTANT ASSETS UNTIL YOU DIE

The majority of people who come to my Success with Trusts seminars have been told of the importance of having a will leaving assets to loved ones personally. Very few advisors tell you that one major defect of a will is that it cannot protect your assets because it does not work until you die. By then, you have lost what the risks of life are going to take from you. Even on death, the government may tax you again with estate duty (as in the United Kingdom or the United States), or capital gains tax (as in Australia).

YOUR WILL MAKES YOUR LOVED ONES WEALTHIER, OFTEN LATER IN LIFE

When you die, your will makes your loved ones personally wealthier. This is often later in their lives, which means your assets are again exposed to risk. How can they totally protect those assets? If you have not taught them that they need a trust, it is not likely that they will form a trust.

Robert's sudden death from a stroke in 1999 left his estate to his wife Barbara, then aged 50. Before he died, they were worth $100,000 net (which in New Zealand could have been gifted to a trust over eight years at $27,000 per year each without gift duty). It would have been easy to have achieved their objectives had they put an asset protection plan in place then. As Barbara said, 'I heard your ads for trust seminars, and Robert and I read your book *Trusts*. We intended to form a trust but simply kept putting it off. As a result of Robert's death I received his life assurance payout of $400,000, and death benefits payable under his superannuation scheme of $250,000.' Her wealth literally increased overnight to $1,050,000. In New Zealand this sum can be gifted by Barbara to a trust over 39 years at $27,000 per year, each without gift duty. 'Why didn't my lawyer explain this to me when he prepared my will? Now I cannot finish my gifting until 89.' However, while it would have been much easier to assist her before Robert's death, she has now transferred all her assets to a trust to protect them as best she can. Her children will inherit trusts with assets in them, and not assets exposed to risk. She is now persuading her children to start asset protection plans so they too can plan to avoid these unnecessary risks.

Your loved ones inherit, regardless of their personal circumstances

Your will gives your trustees no ability to use their common sense. It forces the trustees to pay the inheritance to the named beneficiary regardless of their circumstances. You cannot change your will if you have lost your mental faculties. When you write your will you cannot foresee the circumstances your loved ones will be in when you die or whether they will benefit in the way in which you hope they will.

Joe made a will leaving all of his assets to his wife Mary if she survived him, and if not to his three children, Bill, Jolene and Jasmine. Mary made a will leaving all her assets to Joe if he survived her, and if not, to the three children. At age 78 Joe suffered dementia, lost the power to make a will, and had to be placed in long-term geriatric care. When Mary died, because she had not changed her will, Joe inherited her estate. $100,000 of Joe's assets were eaten up by long-term geriatric care costs. When Joe died, Bill's third of the estate passed to the Official Assignee for payment to his creditors as his business had failed and he had been declared bankrupt.

If Joe had used his will to leave his assets to a trust, the trustees would have kept Bill's share in trust until he was discharged from bankruptcy. Joe's wish that Bill benefit from his estate was not achieved because Joe failed to plan for the worst.

SUMMARY

→ By failing to plan, many lose control over what happens if risks occur. The risks of life then control what happens. Many such risks are easy to plan to avoid.

5

SUCCESS THROUGH WILLS LEAVING ASSETS TO A TRUST

Nothing succeeds like success.

ALEXANDRE DUMAS

SUCCESS THROUGH YOUR WILL LEAVING
ALL ASSETS TO A TRUST

Patrick and Melissa began their asset protection plan at age 75. They had accumulated over $2 million of assets, most of which were owned by Patrick. They had procrastinated about a trust for a good seven years, before finally, and with some apprehension, telling me to go ahead. They equalised their assets with a matrimonial property agreement, which in New Zealand is necessary to avoid gift duty on gifts between husband and wife. Each set up a trust and sold one half of their total assets to that trust, and each made a will leaving all their assets to the trust which they had formed.

Without warning, Patrick died one week later. Melissa now realises that, 'Because of his will, Patrick's gifting was completed on his death, and the assets owned by him outside the trust passed to the trust. One half of our assets are now one hundred percent safe. I did not realise how well it would work.'

Melissa still has to complete her gifting at $27,000 per year, and probably does not have time to do so completely. However, the result achieved is far better than the situation which would have occurred if Melissa had inherited Patrick's wealth. As she now points out, 'When I die my two daughters will inherit a trust each, with half the assets in each. They will then be the sole trustee of one of the trusts. They will get over $1 million each. I am so pleased that nobody will be able to take a cent from them.'

In contrast, Hamish and Joy, who were 55 and 54 respectively, continued to procrastinate about trusts. Their main reason was that their family lawyer had told them that because their assets were only worth $1 million they did not need a trust. In his opinion the chances of estate duty being reinstated were not great, and that all they needed to do was to update their wills.

Hamish died in 1996. Most assets were jointly owned and passed to Joy as the survivor. The rest of the assets passed to Joy as the beneficiary of Hamish's will. Joy told me, 'Overnight I owned not only our $1 million worth of assets but also the life assurance payment of $600,000 paid under Hamish's superannuation scheme.' She was angry when I pointed out that the total wealth of $1.6 million dollars would take her 59 years to gift to the trust at $27,000 per year. Joy will now finish her gifting at age 114 (an unlikely event).

If Hamish and Joy had planned as Patrick and Melissa had, the trust would have been the nominated beneficiary of the life payout under the superannuation scheme. Additionally, the balance of $500,000 lent by Hamish to the trust would have been wiped out on Hamish's death as his will would have left the assets to the trust.

If all assets are owned by the trust (and in the case of couples no longer pass on the death of the first to the survivor), a will leaving all assets to the trust concludes all incomplete gifting at the date of your death. This puts all assets still owned by you personally at the date of your death into the trust. After your death, the assets are then one hundred percent safe and can be kept safe for the beneficiaries of the trust. The assets are safe in the trust until they are paid to the beneficiaries.

If you do not plan you need to be careful where you die. In some countries, the government will try to tax you again. In New Zealand there is no estate duty payable on your death. In the United Kingdom and the United States of America, if you own assets at the date of your death then, depending upon the extent of your assets, estate duty may be incurred. In Australia capital gains tax is payable on your death.

SUCCESS THROUGH YOUR LOVED ONES LEAVING INHERITANCES TO A TRUST

On Wendy's death at the age of 82, her estate, worth $1.5 million, was shared equally by her sons David and Ross, as stipulated in her will. Both David and Ross had accumulated reasonable assets. David, aged 51, had net assets in his name worth $532,000. Ross, aged 44, had net assets in his name worth $2.5 million. In both cases, it will take them 28 years to gift the $750,000 inheritance before they can start gifting their own wealth.

If Wendy had formed a trust and left her assets to that trust David and Ross would not have had any gifting to do and the inheritance would have been one hundred percent safe. They could have inherited trusts.

If parents and other relatives leave what would have been your inheritance to a trust that you have set up, you inherit nothing and nothing can be taken from you. The trust inherits and the inheritance is one hundred percent safe. Better still, if your parents or other loved ones form a trust, on their death 'their' trust can transfer the 'inheritance' to the trust which you have set up.

SUCCESS THROUGH YOUR LOVED ONES INHERITING A TRUST

If your loved ones inherit a trust with assets in it, the trust's assets are never theirs and cannot be taken from them. On your death, your loved ones can become the sole trustees of the trust inherited by them, and in that capacity in charge of the trust.

SUMMARY

✦ By simply changing your wills and relatives' wills to leave assets to trusts, and by loved ones inheriting trusts with assets in them rather than assets exposed to risk, the inherited assets are one hundred percent safe. Why gamble with wills leaving assets to loved ones? It makes no sense to do so.[1]

6

SUCCESS THROUGH RECORDING AND UPDATING YOUR OBJECTIVES

The best way to make your dreams come true is to wake up.

PAUL VALERY

WHAT ARE YOUR IMPORTANT OBJECTIVES?

Each of us has different objectives. Most of those who come to see me have been to one of my Success with Trusts seminars, and are aware of the risks which could prevent them from achieving their important objectives.

One of my young, single business clients told me, 'I want to protect my house from being taken from me as a result of my high risk business failing or my entering into a future relationship. I have already lost half a house due to failing to protect it before my first marriage, and do not want to make the same mistake again.'

A married couple wanted to ensure that the assets they were building up were protected from all possible claims for the long-term benefit of the two of them and their three young children. They told me, 'Our concern is that if one of us dies we do not want any new partner to receive the assets that we have built up together. We want them to remain intact for the benefit of the survivor, and on the survivor's death to be used for the benefit of our children and grandchildren.'

A 70-year-old widow wanted to ensure that her major asset, a valuable house, was safe. 'I am concerned that in the event of me needing long-term geriatric care there may be nothing left over for my three children. I also want my children to inherit my assets in a form that is safe from claims by their partners or others. They all appear to be in happy relationships, but you never know nowadays do you?'

Unless we identify and record our objectives, it is not possible to plan to achieve them. The first part of asset protection planning is to record your objectives.

HOW TO DECIDE ON AND RECORD
YOUR IMPORTANT OBJECTIVES

The following section shows the asset protection plan questionnaire that I use. It covers the information needed for a successful asset protection plan. To plan successfully you need to plan for both the best and worst possible scenarios. An asset protection plan is of no use if it does not cover worst case possibilities. Make sure that you do not attempt to create a perfect plan. This usually results in matters being relegated to the 'too hard basket', as there is no such thing as perfection.

What is important is that you put your present wishes on paper so that if you die or become incapacitated next week, others know what your wishes are. If you change your mind you can, of course, change your wishes.

ASSET PROTECTION PLAN QUESTIONNAIRE
© Ross Holmes Limited

The questionnaire on pages 55–61 should take no longer than two hours to complete. If it takes longer, you are probably making it too hard by attempting to make it perfect. In reality it is no harder than gathering the information needed for a decent will. While none of us likes thinking about our own death, we simply have no option but to do so. Detailed instructions on how to complete this form start on page 60. You may find it easier to enlarge the questionnaire on a photocopier before filling it in.

To: Ross Holmes Limited P.O. Box 33009, Takapuna. Facsimile: 64-9-415-0098 Email rossholmes@rossholmes.co.nz

Information required	First person	Second person (and relationship to first person)
Name	Full Name:	Full Name:
	Occupation:	Occupation:
Address	Flat/Street No:	Flat/Street No:
	Street:	Street:
	Suburb/City and post code:	Suburb/City and postcode:
Personal IRD numbers ESSENTIAL!!!!!		
Phone, fax and email details	Home Phone:	Home Phone:
	Home Fax:	Home Fax:
	Business Phone:	Business Phone:
	Business Fax:	Business Fax:
	Mobile Phone:	Mobile Phone:
Email addresses	Home Email:	Home Email:
	Business Email:	Business Email:
Date of birth	Day/Month/Year:	Day/Month/Year:
Marriage details	Date of Marriage:	Place of Marriage:
Childrens full names, occupation, address, and date of birth	First Child: Full Name:	First Child: Full Name:
	Date of Birth:	Date of Birth:
	Occupation:	Occupation:
	Address:	Address:
	Second Child: Full Name:	Second Child: Full Name:
	Date of Birth:	Date of Birth:
	Occupation:	Occupation:
	Address:	Address:
	Third Child: Full Name:	Third Child: Full Name:
	Date of Birth:	Date of Birth:
	Occupation:	Occupation:
	Address:	Address:
	Fourth Child: Full Name:	Fourth Child: Full Name:
	Date of Birth:	Date of Birth:
	Occupation:	Occupation:
	Address:	Address:
Health	Do You Have Any Serious Health Problems? □ Yes □ No If yes please give details:	Do You Have Any Serious Health Problems? □ Yes □ No If yes please give details:
Bankers for the trust	Name of Bank:	Name of Bank:
	Branch:	Branch:
	Address of Bank:	Address of Bank:
	Phone Number:	Phone Number:
	Fax Number:	Fax Number:
	Email:	Email:
Accountants	Full name:	Full name:

	Name of Firm:	Name of Firm:
	Address:	Address:
	Phone Number:	Phone Number:
	Fax Number:	Fax Number:
	Email:	Email:
Financial Advisors	Full name:	Full name:
	Name of Firm:	Name of Firm:
	Address:	Address:
	Phone Number:	Phone Number:
	Fax Number:	Fax Number:
	Email:	Email:
Full names, residence, and occupations of guardians of your infant children after your death	Full names: Occupation: City of Residence: If more than one person names of others: Full names: Occupation: City of Residence	Full names: Occupation: City of Residence: If more than one person names of others: Full names: Occupation: City of Residence:
Life support	Do you wish the life support system to be turned off if there is no hope? ☐ Yes ☐ No	Do you wish the life support system to be turned off if there is no hope? ☐ Yes ☐ No
Your wishes as to funeral arrangements and organ donation	☐ Buried ☐ Cremated	☐ Buried ☐ Cremated
	Do you wish to donate organs? ☐ Yes ☐ No If yes do you want any restrictions: ☐ Yes ☐ No If yes details:	Do you wish to donate organs? ☐ Yes ☐ No If yes do you want any restrictions: ☐ Yes ☐ No If yes details:
What are your important objectives? (attach details)		
What risks are of concern to you:	Claims by future partners: ☐ Yes ☐ No Business failure or creditor protection: ☐ Yes ☐ No Geriatric care costs: ☐ Yes ☐ No Estate duty or capital gains tax: ☐ Yes ☐ No Protection for children against risks: ☐ Yes ☐ No Other: ☐ Yes ☐ No Please give details:	Claims by future partners: ☐ Yes ☐ No Business failure or creditor protection: ☐ Yes. ☐ No Geriatric care costs: ☐ Yes ☐ No Estate duty or capital gains tax: ☐ Yes ☐ No Protection for children against risks: ☐ Yes ☐ No Other: ☐ Yes ☐ No Please give details:

Do you accept the following?	A will gives you no protection against the risks of life, as it does not work until you die: □ Yes □ No Personal ownership of property gives you no protection against the risks of life: □ Yes □ No Only an asset protection plan with a trust can protect you against the risks of life: □ Yes □ No For a trust to be successful it must have detailed running instructions: □ Yes □ No An asset protection plan must be prepared by a specialist: □ Yes □ No	A will gives you no protection against the risks of life, as it does not work until you die: □ Yes □ No Personal ownership of property gives you no protection against the risks of life: □ Yes □ No Only an asset protection plan with a trust can protect you against the risks of life: □ Yes □ No For a trust to be successful it must have detailed running instructions: □ Yes □ No An asset protection plan must be prepared by a specialist: □ Yes □ No
Do you have any concerns about trusts? If so please specify (use another sheet if necessary):		
Name(s) of trust(s) You can have any name you wish. You have to remember it.	Name of Trust:	Name of Trust:
Trustees of Trust now Full names, place of residence, and occupations	You □ Yes □ No Your Spouse □ Yes □ No Children □ Yes □ No If yes which of the children are to be appointed: All □ Yes □ No Some □ Yes □ No If some which one(s): Other(s) □ Yes □ No If others who:	You □ Yes □ No Your Spouse □ Yes □ No Children □ Yes □ No If yes which of the children are to be appointed: All □ Yes □ No Some □ Yes □ No If some which one(s): Other(s) □ Yes □ No If others who:
Trustees of Trust and your will after your death Full names, place of residence, and occupations	Your Spouse □ Yes □ No Children □ Yes □ No If yes which of the children are to be appointed: All □ Yes □ No Some □ Yes □ No If some which one(s): Other(s) □ Yes □ No If others who:	Your Spouse □ Yes □ No Children □ Yes □ No If yes which of the children are to be appointed: All □ Yes □ No Some □ Yes □ No If some which one(s): Other(s) □ Yes □ No If others who:
Property attorneys after your incapacity Full names, place of residence, and occupations of property attorneys	Your Spouse □ Yes □ No First/second/third Children □ Yes □ No If yes which of the children are to be appointed: All □ Yes □ No First/second/third Some □ Yes □ No If some which one(s): First/second/third Other(s) □ Yes □ No If others who: First/second/third Are they all to act together: □ Yes □ No If they are not all to act together please mark the order in which they are to act above	Your Spouse □ Yes □ No First/second/third Children □ Yes □ No If yes which of the children are to be appointed: All □ Yes □ No First/second/third Some □ Yes □ No If some which one(s): First/second/third Other(s) □ Yes □ No If others who: First/second/third Are they all to act together: □ Yes □ No If they are not all to act together please mark the order in which they are to act above

Welfare attorneys to look after your welfare if you are incapacitated Full names, place of residence, and occupations. Only one can act at a time	Your Spouse ☐ Yes ☐ No First/second/third Children ☐ Yes ☐ No If yes which of the children are to be appointed: All ☐ Yes ☐ No First/second/third Some ☐ Yes ☐ No If some which one(s): First/second/third

Other(s) ☐ Yes ☐ No If others who: | | Your Spouse ☐ Yes ☐ No First/second/third Children ☐ Yes ☐ No If yes which of the children are to be appointed: All ☐ Yes ☐ No First/second/third Some ☐ Yes ☐ No If some which one(s): First/second/third

Other(s) ☐ Yes ☐ No If others who: | | |
If you die who do you want the Trust assets to go to and if more than one the percentages (attach a list)	Your Spouse ☐ Yes First/second/third Children ☐ Yes Other(s) ☐ Yes	☐ No ☐ No ☐ No	Your Spouse ☐ Yes First/second/third Children ☐ Yes Other(s) ☐ Yes	☐ No ☐ No ☐ No	
In the case of a couple on the death of both of you who do you want the Trust assets to go to and if more than one the percentages (attach a list)	Children ☐ Yes Other(s) ☐ Yes If others specify who:	☐ No ☐ No	Children ☐ Yes Other(s) ☐ Yes If others specify who:	☐ No ☐ No	
Age at which to benefit	☐ 20 ☐ 21 ☐ 25 ☐ 30 ☐ Other - Specify		☐ 20 ☐ 21 ☐ 25 ☐ 30 ☐ Other - Specify		
How are they to benefit? (attach details for each beneficiary)	Compulsory trust ☐ Yes Optional trust ☐ Yes Inherit personally ☐ Yes	☐ No ☐ No ☐ No	Compulsory trust ☐ Yes Optional trust ☐ Yes Inherit personally ☐ Yes	☐ No ☐ No ☐ No	

Income Details:
Do you have: (Please tick)
Self employed income: $
Interest and dividend income: $
Employee income: $

Details of assets you wish to sell to your family trust(s) i.e. all assets which will increase in value:
Please complete one list each in the case of couples - show clearly which assets are jointly owned and which are owned separately

Unit Trusts and Shares: Name of Company/Trust Manager Certificate number/Reference number Number of Shares/Units: Current Value of Shares/Units: NZ$ Date of valuation:	Attach details
Life insurance policies: (the same details for each policy) The insurance company's full name: Address: Policy number(s): Policy owner(s): Life(s) assured: Current surrender value(s) of the policy: $	
Superannuation Details: Company name: Address: Owned by: Policy Number Surrender Value $	

Term deposit account details: Name of Bank: Address: Account Number(s) and amount on deposit: 1. 2. 3. Current Account Balance(s) 1. $ 2. $ 3. $		
Other Assets: (Please list with market values) 1. 2. 3. 4. 5.		
Liabilities: (Please list) Overdrafts: Who with? Amount Owing $...................... Personal Loans: Who with? Amount Owing $...................... Credit Cards: Who with? Limit $..................... Amount Owing $...................... **Others:** Tax Owing Amount Owing $...................... Accounts owing Amount Owing $...................... Guarantees Amount Owing $......................		
Properties: Your family home Address: Current Value $ Latest government valuation $ Certificate of title number and registry: Date you purchased property:	**Is there a mortgage against the title:**□ Yes □ No □ Fixed interest □ Floating □ Flexi Credit What is the penalty for early repayment if the Trust purchases the property?: $ Name of lender: Address: Amount owed to lender $ The property the loan relates to is:	Attach copies

Properties: Rental property 1
Address:
 	
Current Value $
Latest government valuation $
Certificate of title number and registry:
Date you purchased property:
In the event of a tax loss on rental properties:
Amount of the annual tax loss $
When the property is likely to run at a profit:
Is there any other income from investments being
transferred to the Trust which can offset that -
                          loss?Yes/No
Taxation benefits on depreciation recovered
What is the total taxation benefits on depreciation
recovered for the properties to be sold to the Trust(s)?:
$
How much relates to chattels?: $
    Is the market value of the chattels greater than the book
                    value of the chattels?Yes/No
If yes, then this amount will be added to your income and
taxed in the year of sale.
Possession date for sale of rental properties:
Attach the same details for all other properties
	Is there a mortgage against the title:□ Yes □ No
	□ Fixed interest □ Floating □ Flexi Credit
	What is the penalty for early repayment if the Trust purchases
	the property?: $
	Name of lender:
	Address:
	Amount owed to lender $
	The property the loan relates to is:	

In the case of Private Companies we need the following information:	
A copy of the last annual accounts	
The number of shares in the company in total:	
The number of shares owned by each of you:	
The full names of all directors:	
The full names of all shareholders:	
Are there any losses carried forward for the company. □ Yes □ No	
Is the company a Loss attributing Qualifying Company □ Yes □ No	
Are there any retained earnings? □ Yes □ No	
The date of the last accounts for the company:	
Are monthly profit and loss accounts prepared for the company? □ Yes □ No	
How much does the company owe you as the shareholders? $	
Are there any outside shareholders? □ Yes □ No	
If yes please detail their full names:	
If so do they agree to the transfer of shares to the Trust? □ Yes □ No	
Are there any substantial risks of the company being sued? □ Yes □ No	
Are these risks adequately covered by insurance? □ Yes □ No	
What income is paid to you as the shareholders after expenses and before tax? $	
What is the commercial market rate salary which they would pay someone else to do your job? $	
What dividends have been received by you as the shareholders in the last financial year? $	
Do the shareholders charge the company interest on their shareholders loan accounts,	
and if so how much in the last year? $	
What is the value of the plant and equipment owned by the Company? $	
Is any of the plant and equipment leased from others? □ Yes □ No	
GST	
Are the you GST registered in respect of the properties or business to be sold?Yes/No	
Your GST registration number:	
Your GST return frequency: Monthly/Two monthly/Six monthly	
The date on which your next GST period ends:	

Taxation questions for properties:

Were any of the properties purchased with the intention or purpose of re-sale? **(Section CD1(2)(a))** Yes/No

If yes, was the property occupied primarily and principally either as your residence or your business premises? (Section CD1(3)) Yes/No

If yes, has there been a regular pattern of buying and selling the residence or business premises? (proviso in Section CD1(3)) Yes/No

Subdivisions

Regardless of your occupation of the client, have any of the properties commenced to be developed or divided into lots within 10 years of acquisition and was the work of more than a minor nature? **(Section CD 1(2)(f))** Yes/No

If yes, was the work for the use in and for the purpose of your residence or your business premises or the deriving of rents? (provisos to s.CD1(2)(f)) Yes/No

If no, is the land less than 4,500 sq.m and occupied or erected primarily and principally either as your residence? (Section CD1(6)) Yes/No

If no, was the land used for subdivision primarily and principally for the purpose of a farming or agricultural business, can it be worked as an economic unit and will the farming or agricultural business continue? (Section CD1(7)) Yes/No

Did the subdivision involve significant expenditure? **(Section CD1(2)(g))** Yes/No

If yes, is the land less than 4,500 sq.m and occupied or erected primarily and principally either as your residence? (Section CD1(6))Yes/No

If no, was the land used for subdivision primarily and principally for the purpose of a farming or agricultural business, can it be worked as an economic unit and will the farming or agricultural business continue? (Section CD1(7)) Yes/No

Property developers and those associated with property developers only

Are you, or an associated person client, a dealer in land and were any of the properties acquired for the purpose of that business or purchased less than 10 years ago? **(Section CD(1)(2) (b))** Yes/No

If yes, was the property occupied primarily and principally either as your residence or your business premises? (Section CD1(3)) Yes/No

If yes, has there been a regular pattern of buying and selling the residence for business premises? (proviso in Section CD1(3)) Yes/No

Were you, or an associated person of the client, a builder at the date of acquisition of any of the properties and have you made improvements to the land of more than a minor nature and was, either, the land acquired for the purpose of the building business, or, the improvements carried out not less than 10 years ago? **(Section CD1(2)(d))** Yes/No

If yes, was the property occupied or erected primarily and principally either as your residence or your business premises? (Section CD1(3)) Yes/No

If yes, has there been a regular pattern of buying and selling the residence for business premises? (proviso in Section CD1(3)) Yes/No

For any of the properties has there been some permitted change or likelihood of such a change in the use of the land since its acquisition? **Section (CD1(2)(e))** Yes/No

If yes, was the property a re-zoned farm sold as a farm and for reasons unconnected with the re-zoning? (Section CD1(4)) Yes/No

Are you, or an associated person, in the business of developing or subdividing and were any of the properties acquired for that business or acquired less than 10 years ago and was the subdivision work of more than a minor nature? **(Section CD1(2)(c))** Yes/No

If yes, was the property occupied or erected primarily and principally either as your residence or your business premises? (Section CD1(3)) Yes/No

If yes, has there been a regular pattern of buying and selling the residence for business premises? (proviso in Section CD1(3)) Yes/No

Oddoc chart3

COMPLETION OF THE QUESTIONNAIRE

Unless your expert knows all about you they cannot tailor an asset protection plan to achieve your objectives. This not only involves knowledge of your objectives, assets and liabilities, but also a knowledge of your income and businesses.

Preparing an asset protection plan and trust involves far more than filling in a few names on a standard trust deed form. Advisors who instantly prepare trust deeds by simply filling in a few blanks are ripping you off. Frequently, such trust deeds are not worth the paper on which they are written.

Guardians of your infant children

Guardianship is the right to make important decisions regarding the upbringing of a child, for example, deciding his or her educational needs. Legally, both parents of a child are his or her guardians. In New Zealand, Section 7 of the Guardianship Act 1968 permits the father or the mother of a child (including an unborn child) to appoint any person to be a guardian of the child after his or her death, through their will.

Life support

In New Zealand, Australia and the United Kingdom, there is no specific legal provision dealing with disconnection of life support systems. Your wishes as to the disconnection of life support systems have no legal force in these countries, but can be shown by your loved ones to the doctor so he/she can take them into account when making such decisions, if this is legally possible.

Some countries/states (such as some states in the USA) permit you to decide whether the life support system that you are connected to should be turned off or to decline specific medical treatment. These countries/states make provision for the document that needs to be completed when expressing such wishes.

Your wishes for your funeral

In addition, you can include requests as to where you are to be buried, or where and how your ashes are to be scattered. Some people like to detail the funeral service they wish to have. Some provide for a function after the funeral.

Organ donations

If you are an organ donor, you need to specify which organs you wish to be donated on your death. The following possibilities need to be considered:

❈ Any needed organs, tissues, or parts;

❈ Any needed organs, tissues, or parts except my *(insert body parts not to be donated)*;

❈ The following organs, tissues, or parts only *(insert organs to be donated)*.

If you do wish to be an organ donor, for what purpose are the organs to be donated? *(Select one)*:

❈ Any purpose authorised by law;

❈ The following purposes *(Select one)*: transplantation, research, therapy, education.

Do you wish your organs, tissues, or parts to be given, if possible, to relatives of yours in the first instance, and if this is not possible to any other person?

Name(s) of trust(s)

You can use any name you wish for your trust. You have to remember it. My recommendation is that you use your own names unless there is a special name you want for sentimental reasons. The name gives no secrecy, as everyone with whom the trust deals will know who the trustees are.

Trustees of the trust during your lifetime

In essence, the trustees must be the people who are genuinely making decisions.[1] Do not appoint anyone who will merely act as a rubber stamp. To do so will damage credibility and probably result in the trust or the trust's transactions being invalid. A trust or a trust transaction which is not genuine may be a sham, that is, a pretence, and is therefore invalid.[2]

The trustees of the trust will normally be yourself and any other person whom you wish to involve in making the trust's important decisions.

Trustees of your will and trustees of the trust after your death or mental incapacity

After your death, the trustees of your trust and the trustees of your will should always be the same people, for consistency. These people will make important decisions as to the distribution of the trust's assets.

For those of you who are single, who is to look after your assets if you become incapacitated or die? If that person is dead or incapacitated, who is to replace them? For couples, your partner can be the sole trustee if this is what you wish. However, if your partner is dead or incapacitated, who is to take over as the replacement? If you and any partner have died and you have children, are they old enough and responsible enough to be the backstop trustees? If the answer is yes, they should be appointed. If the answer is no, but the children are old enough, they could be appointed in conjunction with someone you consider responsible enough. This involves the children in decisions so they will not feel left out. The trusts I set up provide that decisions of trustees must be unanimous and children cannot outvote the other trustee.

Unless the law provides a minimum age for the appointment of trustees, trustees must be old enough to legally enter into contracts. This age varies from country to country and state to state. In New Zealand it is age 18.

Property attorneys after your incapacity

In New Zealand, the United Kingdom and some provinces in Canada, some states in Australia and the United States of America, it is possible to prepare what is known as an enduring power of attorney regarding property. This is similar to a normal power of attorney, in that it gives people the right to sign documents on your behalf relating to all of your property or specified parts of your property (but not the trust's assets which are no longer yours and are dealt with by the trustees of the trust). It can be used after you become mentally incapacitated, which is why it is called 'enduring'. In some jurisdictions (such as New Zealand), an enduring power of attorney can be used as a normal power of attorney if it provides for this.

Such property attorneys (depending upon the law in your country/state) can be appointed to act jointly and severally, that is, any one of them, or one followed by another. You can provide for backstop property attorneys, and need to detail the batting order in which they are to be appointed. If the backstops are children, will they be upset if they are named out of age order? In New Zealand such attorneys must be aged 20 or over.

Welfare attorneys to look after your welfare if you are incapacitated

In New Zealand and some Australian states it is possible to prepare what is known as an enduring power of attorney as to welfare. It gives appointed people the right to make welfare-type decisions on your behalf (such as health care decisions and admission to hospital) if you become mentally incapacitated. Welfare attorneys need to be humane.

In New Zealand, only one person at a time can be a welfare attorney. However, you can provide for backstop welfare attorneys, and need to detail the batting order in which they are to be appointed. Once again, if the backstops are children, will they be upset if they are named out of age order? In New Zealand such attorneys must be aged 20 or over.

Your beneficiaries

Who do you want to benefit on your death? If they are not alive then who is the backstop? At what age and in what form do you want them to benefit? Do you want them to inherit a trust with assets in it, rather than inheriting assets personally? This is my recommendation as this way the assets are one hundred percent safe from attacks by others.

In the case of older people, what is going to happen to the assets if they inherit them personally? Is it not better for the assets to remain in the trust with the 'older' people being paid out money as they require it, so that what is in the trust is never theirs? In this way, it cannot be taken from them.

SUCCESS THROUGH UPDATING YOUR OBJECTIVES

After completing your asset protection plan, if your objectives or circumstances change it is essential that your asset protection planning documents are updated to reflect such changes. If they are not, the plan will not achieve your objectives.

If the law changes in a way that affects your asset protection plan, your asset protection planning documents must be amended to cover or protect against such changes. Your advisor must make a commitment to inform you whenever this is necessary.[3]

SUMMARY

→ Unless your objectives are identified and recorded, you cannot plan to achieve them. In reality, this is no harder than gathering the information needed for a decent will. While none of us likes thinking about our own death, we simply have no option but to do so.

→ Unless your expert knows all about you they cannot tailor an asset protection plan to achieve your objectives. This not only involves knowledge of your objectives, assets and liabilities, but also a knowledge of your income and businesses.

→ After completing your asset protection plan, if your objectives or circumstances change it is essential that your asset protection planning documents are updated to reflect such changes. If the law changes in a way which affects your asset protection plan your asset protection planning documents must be amended to cover or protect against such changes.

7

SUCCESS THROUGH PLANNING NOW

He who waits for roast duck to fly into his mouth must wait a very, very long time.

CHINESE PROVERB

SUCCESS THROUGH ACTION,
NOT PROCRASTINATION

We are all good at procrastinating. This is particularly the case with asset protection planning or estate planning (as some people call it). Estate planning sounds too much like you have to be old or almost dying before it is needed. Asset protection planning is, as you now know, all about protecting your assets as you get them and stopping unwanted parties from taking them from you and your loved ones. Planning in advance always works best.

If you keep putting off your asset protection planning, what is going to happen? Firstly, you are going to get older. Secondly, as you get older your assets go up in value because of inflation, and you get richer as you accumulate more assets. Thirdly, as you get older and richer it gets harder to gift your assets.

Amelia and James were 54 when they came to one of my Success with Trusts seminars in 1999. Like many of my clients, they did not understand what could be achieved with an asset protection plan. They had accumulated assets with a net value of $3.8 million, of which $2.5 million had been gained over the previous ten years from a very successful business. As with so many of my clients, they had been advised by their lawyer that there was no need to set up a trust. James said, 'In 1989 we had a great opportunity to set up a new business. We had a house worth about $600,000 and $200,000 of other savings. Our family lawyer assisted us with the legal work. We asked him if we needed a trust. He told us that at 44 we were too young and that we did not have enough assets to need a trust.' Had Amelia and James started their asset protection plan in 1989 it would have taken them fifteen years to gift their $800,000 worth of assets at $27,000 per year in New Zealand. 'We feel extremely disappointed that our lawyer gave us such poor advice. It will

> now take us 70 years to complete gifting our assets.' In New Zealand, Amelia and James cannot fully complete their gifting in their lifetime. However, in 1999, they commenced their asset protection plan, selling their assets to the trusts and pegging their wealth at the IOU of $1.9 million each which the trust gave them in exchange for the assets. Future increases in value will belong to the trusts. They have wills leaving all assets to the trusts. After their deaths, their two children will each inherit a trust, each with an equal value of assets.
>
> Amelia and James realise that, 'Even starting now we are going to achieve our aims a lot better than if we did nothing. It was really scary when we realised that in the past we had no real protection.'

In Australia and other countries with capital gains tax and stamp duty, it can be very expensive to restructure once you have accumulated such wealth. The earlier you start planning the fewer problems there are. If you do not start an asset protection plan now and you lose your mental faculties, there is no second chance. If you do not start an asset protection plan now and you die there is no second chance.

SUCCESS FOR COUPLES THROUGH PLANNING WHEN YOU ARE BOTH ALIVE

In the case of couples, sit down and add up how much the survivor will be worth if one of you died tomorrow. Don't forget to add in payouts under life assurance policies and superannuation schemes.

In countries such as New Zealand, the United Kingdom and the United States, which impose gift duty, the survivor's opportunities to gift their new wealth are much more limited than those the couple previously had together.

SUCCESS THROUGH NOT PLANNING AT THE LAST MINUTE

The Chinese proverb at the beginning of this chapter sums it all up: 'He who waits for a roast duck to fly into his mouth must wait a very, very long time.' By leaving matters to the last minute you run the risk of dying or becoming incapacitated or growing older and wealthier. Why risk disaster and reduce or lose your opportunities to plan?

Why put it off? You need to plan to succeed in all areas, including asset protection planning. Failing to plan is planning to fail — a result none of us wants.

SUCCESS THROUGH POSITIVE THOUGHT — THE GOVERNMENT WILL NOT OUTLAW TRUSTS

I have been practising law since 1973 and people have been saying since well before then that the government will change the rules and that there is therefore no point in forming a trust. This has not been true at any time. Those who have believed that the government will change the rules and have done nothing have suffered. Those who have acted and protected their assets have succeeded.

Initially, the wealthy established trusts to protect their land against taxes on death. The usefulness of trusts has expanded greatly since that time. Despite the long history of trusts, none of the countries in the world which have trusts as part of their legal systems have attacked trusts. Nor will that ever happen.

In a number of countries, including Australia and the United Kingdom, trusts have been used by the rich to exploit tax loopholes.

Naturally, governments will close such loopholes from time to time, as has occurred recently in Australia and the United Kingdom. However, this is not an attack on trusts, but an understandable attempt by governments to preserve tax bases.

Many countries, including New Zealand, Australia and the United Kingdom, have introduced anti-avoidance measures that relate to qualifications for state benefits. These measures are an attempt to prevent people disposing of assets to qualify for benefits. Such measures apply both to those with and without trusts, and these measures are needed as most people attempt to avoid them through means such as gifting assets to children.[1] As a matter of common sense, any anti-avoidance measures have to apply across the board to all types of avoidance activity and not just to trusts.

A look at political party websites[2] shows that they have very little interest in trusts, only in the taxation of trusts in countries in which the government has failed in the past to plug tax loopholes. In New Zealand, all significant trust taxation loopholes were plugged in the mid-1980s.

SUMMARY

➔ Procrastinating about your asset protection plan gives you no protection. You are crossing your fingers and hoping that the risks of life will not affect you. What happens is that you get older, as you get older your assets increase in value with inflation, and you get richer as you accumulate more assets. As you get older and richer, your ability to gift the assets is reduced.

➔ You get no second chance if you lose your mental faculties or if you die.

✦ In the case of couples, on the death of one partner the survivor is often much wealthier and gifting will take much longer.

✦ By leaving matters to the last minute your opportunities to plan may be lost or reduced. Why put it off? You have to plan to succeed in all areas, including asset protection planning.[3]

8

THE STEPS TO SUCCESS USING A COMPREHENSIVE ASSET PROTECTION PLAN

I will tell you how to become rich. Close the doors. Be fearful when others are greedy. Be greedy when others are fearful.

WARREN BUFFETT (AGED 21) LECTURING TO A GROUP OF STUDENTS AT COLUMBIA UNIVERSITY

Success through developing a strategy to achieve your objectives

Asset protection planning is just like business and investment planning. We all need a strategy to achieve our objectives. What should it be? How is it going to work? As none of us can afford to gamble with our future, the strategy must not take unnecessary risks with our assets. As discussed earlier, the 'old ways' are not safe ways. Each of us needs to develop a strategy that will help us achieve our objectives. These strategies must be kept simple. If we cannot understand or easily operate them they will not work. The secret is so obvious that most people do not see it. If you have nothing, others have nothing to take from you.

The strategy that I advise my clients to use works — personal poverty and a rich trust. I have practised this strategy and have not had any personal assets for many years. This has had no impact on the borrowing or investment ability of the trusts that I have formed for the benefit of my family.

Long-term clients William and Samantha (see chapter 3) sold the shares in their company and all their properties to the trusts they had established. Their salaries are paid into their personal bank accounts, and used solely for their personal expenditure. They have had no difficulty running the trusts, and the wealth of the trusts has grown substantially. Through a regular gifting programme William and Samantha have now achieved personal poverty and rich trusts.

Their daughters have also had no difficulty running the trusts that their parents set up to protect them. Renee says, 'It has been a piece of cake keeping the records for the trust. Because we started with virtually nothing, it was great having a filing system within a folder with instructions on how to make trustee decisions and how to file things. Mum and Dad wish that they

> had had it this easy when they started buying investments.'
> Cindy is also happy with the situation, because as 'the trust
> owns the house I feel safe. I realise that by being personally
> poor my entire life, the trust's asset protection will succeed one
> hundred percent.'

Unfortunately very few younger people realise the need to start asset protection plans. The younger you start the quicker you get one hundred percent protection.

SUCCESS THROUGH PUTTING IN PLACE A METHOD TO ACHIEVE THAT STRATEGY

A strategy on its own is of limited use. We also need to put in place methods to achieve that strategy. In my own case and that of my clients, the method is also very simple — you spend, the trust invests.

By using your personal bank account for personal expenditure only, and the trust's bank account for investment purchases, investment sales and investment income, your affairs will be simpler than they are now. All investment records are set out in the trust's bank statements instead of being muddled up in your personal bank statements.

In the case of private companies, by using the same discipline and never using the company's bank account for personal expenditure, the company's accounts are simplified. The company is only used for business income and business expenditure, and not for investments. Investments are normally made by the trust so that they are safe from claims by any person who takes proceedings against the company.

SUCCESS THROUGH TAKING TIME TO LOOK AFTER YOUR OWN AFFAIRS

Most of us spend much of our lives looking after others at our places of employment. What I am suggesting is taking the time to look after your own affairs. It is, after all, action and not procrastination that works. Your own affairs are not going to be sorted out if you procrastinate.

SUCCESS THROUGH NOT GETTING BOGGED DOWN WITH DOTTING I'S AND CROSSING T'S

If you get bogged down with dotting i's and crossing t's, what happens? Nothing. You lose sight of your important objectives and fail to achieve them. Unfortunately, there is a lot of misinformation about trusts available, making it difficult to sort fact from fiction.

When you think about it, it is not difficult to understand why. Until recent generations, only the rich were hit by high taxes and high estate/death duties. As a result, only the rich needed the protection of trusts. It followed that only the advisors to the rich needed to know about trusts. What other advisors knew was often passed on by word of mouth, without research. As you will be aware, things often get distorted when passed on by word of mouth.

Just because a non-expert advisor says something does not make it correct. We all need to protect our assets and achieve our objectives. Many advisors do not recognise that this is the case, and most incorrectly believe that very few people need trusts. In the majority of cases this is because those advisors do not regard trusts in the same way as they do insurance policies.

Before forming a trust, you do not need to read as many books as possible on trusts, or take as many opinions as possible from others. All this will do is get you bogged down. You are likely to get totally confused by both the quantity of information and the conflicting advice you receive. What will happen? It will all go into your 'too hard' basket and you will continue to procrastinate.

At the end of the day you are not going to become a trust expert. You are going to have to rely on an expert to take care of dotting i's and crossing t's. Approach the formation of a trust as if you were starting a company. Do not make it too hard. If you are taking advice, make sure it is backed up by reference to case law or legislation. Advice without reference to case law or legislation may well be without value. Also, try to avoid relying on books written by investment planners or non-experts.

WHY A TRUST ON ITS OWN CANNOT SUCCEED

Even if a trust deed is good and the trustees are aware of their legal obligations, what are they going to do with the trust? A trust is not an asset protection plan. It is just a legal document containing rules that the trustees have to follow for the running of the trust — just like a company constitution, or the rules of an incorporated society.

On its own it cannot work successfully. It is a bit like forming a company and not having a business plan. It is the business plan that makes the company succeed, not its constitution (which sets out the rules for the running of the company).

What you need is an asset protection plan — a comprehensive set of documents that gel together to achieve your objectives. The 'keep it simple' principle works best. You and the trustees must understand the asset protection programme and it must meet your objectives. Otherwise it is likely to fail. This is because if you do not understand it, or it is not meeting your objectives, you will be likely to fail to follow the requirements which must be followed for the trust to be effective.

SUCCESS THROUGH A SERIES OF DOCUMENTS WHICH WORK TOGETHER TO ACHIEVE YOUR OBJECTIVES

Step 1

Identify your objectives and develop a strategy designed to minimise the risk of events occurring that could interfere with the achievement of those objectives. I have rarely seen an asset protection plan with such a strategy.

In the case of most of my clients, their objective is simple: personal poverty and a rich trust (for a variety of genuine asset protection reasons). In the case of many settlors, the strategy necessary to achieve those goals is also simple: the trust invests, the settlor spends.

If no such strategy is designed, the trust and other asset protection planning documents are documents with a goal in mind (such as asset protection) but no plan for how to reach that goal. On its own, a trust cannot fully achieve your objectives.

Step 2

Ensure that future increases in asset value belong to the trust. The strategy which I and my clients adopt works — personal poverty and a rich trust. If you have nothing, others have nothing to take from you. We also need to put in place methods to achieve that strategy — you spend, the trust invests. In this way future increases in asset value will belong to the trust.

Step 3

Ensure that the trust, and not you and your loved ones, inherits wealth. This is achieved by you and your loved ones changing your wills to leave assets to the trust.

Step 4

Ensure that your loved ones 'inherit' trusts and not wealth. A trust, when it is properly prepared, contains provisions enabling the transfer of assets to other trusts.

DOCUMENTS REQUIRED AS PART OF YOUR ASSET PROTECTION PLAN

An asset protection plan is a series of documents which gel together to achieve your objectives.

A trust deed on its own is of limited use, and indeed very dangerous. On its own it cannot effectively transfer ownership of your assets to the trust. If you do not effectively transfer ownership of your assets to the trust, they will be treated as still being yours for all purposes. If a comprehensive set of documents that gels together is not prepared, your objectives cannot be fully achieved.

An asset protection plan must include the following documents:

✻ Detailed notes of guidance for the trustees about how to run the trust and keep the trust's records in a creditable manner.

✻ The following, all of which should be prepared by your expert, and which must gel together to achieve your objectives:

— A modern, flexible trust deed.

— A Memorandum of Wishes for the trust. This is a bit like a flowery will, and sets out your wishes for the trust after your death. Beneficiaries should normally 'inherit' trusts with assets in them (totally safe from others) and not assets exposed to risk.

— A minute book, and initial minutes for the trust.

— Draft minutes dealing with future loans, future loan repayments, future asset purchases, future asset sales, income distributions, capital distributions, approval of the annual accounts/taxation return, and approval of the trust's investment plan.

— A trust transaction chart on which to record, in date sequence, a running total of the loan balance owed to you, by recording the initial loan made by you to the trust, the gifts of that loan made by you, future loans by you and loan repayments made to you by the trust.

— Agreements for sale and purchase of property, settlement statements, and transfers.

— Deeds of Acknowledgment of Debt recording the loan(s) made by you to the trust.

— A Deed of Trust for assets declaring that the assets transferred to the trust are held by the trustees in trust for the trust, and are not owned by them personally.

— Deeds of reduction of debt and gift statements evidencing the gifts made by you and others to the trust.

— A new will, normally leaving all of your assets to the trust. The function of a will in an asset protection plan is to complete any gifting not completed by you at the date of your death, and to wipe any loan balance owed to you by the trust at that time.

— Enduring powers of attorney as to property and welfare.

Where possible, the wills of loved ones likely to leave you money or assets should be changed so that they are left to the trust of which you are a beneficiary.

Investment planning advice and business planning must be undertaken.

SUMMARY

→ On its own, a trust cannot work successfully. What you need is an asset protection plan — a comprehensive set of documents, all of which gel together to achieve your objectives.

→ Advisors who have expertise in this area will, with careful planning, be able to establish a trust and prepare the other essential documents, which not only work, but will be more likely to stand up to challenges from agents of the government, future husbands, wives or partners, beneficiaries and others.

→ The old ways are not safe. The strategy that my clients and I adopt works — personal poverty and a rich trust. If you have nothing, others have nothing to take from you.

→ You need to put in place methods to achieve your strategy — you spend, the trust invests. You can lose sight of your important objectives and fail to achieve them if you get bogged down with too much detail.

9

SUCCESS THROUGH USING AN EXPERT TO PREPARE YOUR ASSET PROTECTION PLAN

[An expert is] somebody who is more than fifty miles from home, has no responsibility for implementing the advice he gives, and shows slides.

EDWIN MEESE

AN ASSET PROTECTION PLAN WILL ONLY WORK IF YOU USE AN EXPERT WHO HAS SUCCEEDED

Even if we do decide to plan, we often use our normal advisors — even though they are not experts in asset protection planning. Many asset protection plans fail for this reason. After all, you are planning in case it all turns to custard. Your asset protection plan must work in the worst case scenario.

To learn to plan you must hire the best advisors — experts in their field who have themselves succeeded. Despite the changes in society, many advisors are themselves still attempting to achieve their important objectives in the same old and now unsafe ways. What is scary is that many of the advisors upon whom we rely for our success — accountants, bankers, lawyers, and investment advisors — have themselves not become wealthy. Let's look at some disasters which can and do occur when non-expert advisors prepare trusts on their own without an asset protection plan.

John married Janet in 1989, confident that the house and investments owned by the trust which he had established prior to the relationship was not matrimonial property, and that Janet would get no share of the home if their relationship failed. He even entered a pre-marital agreement that recognised Janet had no claim to the trust's assets.

John told me, 'My normal lawyer had carried out all my legal work well for years. I told him that I was getting married, and he told me to form a trust and enter into a pre-marital contract.' That advice was great. However, John was advised that it was essential that he have an independent trustee. John and his accountant were appointed as trustees of the trust. 'I believed that having an accountant as an independent trustee would ensure that the trust was properly administered.'

John's accountant did not inspect the home prior to signing

the purchase agreement by which the trust agreed to purchase the house. He had seen the valuer's report that John had obtained to fix the sale price. While the house and investments were sold to the trust for their current market value, the independent trustee gave no consideration as to whether the house and other investments were appropriate investments for the trust (and nor did John's lawyer know that this was necessary). The trustees did not obtain any opinion from a share broker or investment advisor.

John did not realise there were any further steps he needed to take apart from signing up. 'I assumed that my lawyer would have told me if I had to do anything else.' Apart from preparing a minute for the purchase of the initial investments, John's lawyer gave him no instructions on the running of the trust, prepared no minute book, and no future draft minutes for the trust's decisions.

'I carried on as before, changing the investments regularly on my own, using the trust's cheque book. I heard nothing over the years from my lawyer.' He met with his accountant once a year to approve and sign the accounts which had been prepared for the trust for the preceding year. 'I assumed, as a result, that there was no need to consult the independent trustee about changes in the trust's investments or payments to beneficiaries. My accountant had, after all, pre-signed trust cheques for that purpose.' John signed minutes prepared by the accountant at the end of each year, treating those payments to beneficiaries as their income (for income splitting purposes).

'Janet left me in 1999. Through her lawyer she claimed that the trust was a sham, that the house and investments were as a result held by the trustees in a resulting trust in my favour, and that she was entitled to 50 percent of the house (but not the other investments which were my separate property). I could not believe that this could happen. I thought it was all watertight.'

The court held that the trust was a sham or invalid for the following reasons:

⚹ There was no intention by John to create a trust. He had acted as if he still owned the trust's assets.

⚹ The independent trustee had not given any consideration as to whether the initial investments of the trust were appropriate, and had therefore not acted honestly and in good faith. There was accordingly no valid purchase by the trust of the home or investments.

⚹ The independent trustee had not taken part in the subsequent investment decisions, or the distributions to beneficiaries, which were all invalid.

⚹ The trust's assets, and the payments to the beneficiaries, were therefore held in a resulting trust for John, the home was the matrimonial home, and Janet was entitled to half of it.

If John had contacted a trust specialist he may have avoided this outcome. The trustees must always act genuinely.

Long-term geriatric care costs

Exactly the same situation would arise if John required long-term geriatric care after age 65. In the event of the relevant government agency (in New Zealand, the Department of Work and Income[1]) treating the trust as a sham and determining that there was a resulting trust back to John, all of the trust's assets (and indeed every payment made out of the trust over the years to the beneficiaries) would belong to John. The assets would have to be used to meet John's long-term geriatric care needs (in New Zealand until the assets are reduced to $15,000, if a person is single) before he would qualify for a residential care subsidy.

Estate duty and inheritance taxes

Again, the same situation would arise if John died and estate duty or inheritance tax had been reintroduced before that time. In the event of the relevant revenue department succeeding in setting aside the trust as a sham, there would be a resulting trust back to

John, with all of the trust's assets (and every payment made out of the trust over the years to the beneficiaries) forming part of John's estate. Estate duty or inheritance tax would be imposed on those assets as part of John's estate, if his estate exceeded estate duty or inheritance tax limits.

In each of these cases, if John had been the sole trustee, and one of a number of beneficiaries, the trust and its transactions would have been valid so long as he, in his capacity as trustee, had acted honestly and in good faith. The minutes prepared by his accountant after the transactions would not have been shams, as they would have recorded what John had decided earlier. The decisions would also have been valid had all trustees genuinely taken part in them.

Asset protection planning and trusts involve complex issues which make quality advice a must, both in relation to the initial establishment of the asset protection plan and trust and its ongoing administration. To prepare and assist in the continuing effectiveness of an asset protection plan involves obtaining and updating a detailed knowledge of the settlor's objectives, businesses, assets, liabilities and income.

Asset protection planning is a highly specialised field. Trust and taxation law are constantly evolving, and change regularly. Your expert must keep up to date with the latest legal developments. It is not safe for advisors to rely upon words or procedures from the precedents which advisors have used in previous years, even if a court has decided that such words or procedures were used successfully in previous decades. As stated by L.J. Lindley,[2]

You must take the [document] which you have to construe and see what it means, and if you come to the conclusion that no trust was intended, you say so, although previous judges have said the contrary on some [document] more or less similar to the one you have to construe.

Asset protection planning advisors must check the accuracy of what they have read or heard. Most seminar papers, articles and books refer to cases, but due to word constraints, do not set out excerpts from those cases which would give the general practitioner the ability to see if the case supports the contentions being made. A general practitioner does not normally have time to carry out the detailed and ongoing research the specialist asset protection planner is required to undertake.

The difficulty with general practitioner advisors forming trusts is that situations such as that faced by John arise when neither the advisor nor their clients are equipped to deal with the situation.

These dangers are frequently covered up until problems arise . By then, it is often too late to cure the problem.

In every case, a trust is set up as part of an asset protection plan in case dangers that could occur do occur. If the asset protection plan does not provide any protection against worst case scenarios occurring, it has not fulfilled its function.

As a result of a failure to use experts, trust litigation is already a growth industry in Australia and England, and will become one elsewhere. It is not humanly possible for advisors to be specialists in all areas of law. No general practitioner doctor would consider carrying out heart surgery. They would refer the patient to a heart specialist to ensure they received the best possible medical treatment. The patient would then return to the GP for their normal medical treatment, thankful for the specialist referral. They are more likely to remain a patient of their GP. For the same reasons, a similar referral system needs to be used in the legal profession when approaching asset protection planning matters.

If your advisor is not an expert, insist that they refer you to someone who is for this part of your legal work. If they are interested in you obtaining the best possible result, they will want to refer you to an expert. They do not need to lose you as a client. I frequently carry out only this part of a client's legal work. A team approach is what is needed, with an asset protection planning specialist, a lawyer and the client's accountant working as a team.

The Trust needs detailed running instructions to make it simple

The 'Achilles heel' of many trusts is that while care is taken in the drafting of the trust deed and the transfer of assets to the trust, many lawyers unwisely take a hands-off approach to the subsequent administration of the trust.

As stated in *Administration of Trusts* (1999),[3] 'the existence of a coherent system of administration is the only way of ensuring that trustees fulfil their duties under the law and avoid liability for breaches of trust'.

In *Topical Trust Issues* (1998)[4] it was observed that:

> *the settlor/trustee will often be the primary individual running a trust, with the other trustees really just 'rubber stamping' the settlor's actions. This can have serious consequences for the validity of a trust if it is subject to close scrutiny. At the risk of being provocative, I would suggest that a great many New Zealand trusts are run in a manner not too dissimilar to the trust in the Rahman case, in which the trust was held to be a sham, in part because of the trustee failing to exercise its own discretion, and the settlor making the decisions. In my opinion, this is the Achilles heel of many trusts. While considerable care is taken in the drafting of the trust deed and the transfer of assets to the trust, many lawyers take a hands-off approach to subsequent administration.*

A substantial part of my time is spent reviewing, and in many cases discarding, trusts which are not prepared as part of a comprehensive asset protection plan, have been incorrectly prepared, and/or have grossly inadequate record keeping systems.

The following example[5] shows the extent of the guidance commonly given.

> *While trusts are relatively informal and do not have any formal reporting requirements, it is usually a good idea to keep a minute book in which can be recorded any decisions which are made during the trust year. Where there are investments, the trust should keep a separate bank account so that income streams can be easily identified . . . Only the trustees may decide on income and capital distributions. They may exercise their powers as they see fit . . . We advise trustees to record their considerations in writing in the minute book and to provide some reasons for their decisions . . . The minute book should be kept as a day-to-day record of the trust, in the same way as a company's minute book is maintained.*

Failure to provide adequate guidance has resulted in the invalidity of the trust itself and invalid trust transactions, even if the trust deed was initially well prepared. What professionals often fail to recognise is that non-professional trustees do not know what is required for a decision of trustees to be valid. Without guidance, they are unlikely to be able to keep adequate minutes. Trustees need to know how to record the decisions of the trust and what trustees should do to ensure their decisions are valid. With practical guidance from day one, these are simple matters.

How are trustees going to piece together the trust's records years later? Frequently they cannot — they may be dead or incapacitated. If they can it is often very time consuming and, as a result, expensive. Many trusts have become a nightmare to run, simply because the advisor gave the trustees no practical operating instructions. A trust will be easy to run if the advisor prepares the following:

- A trust with indexed, practical running instructions.
- A set of tabbed and indexed asset protection planning documents which gel together to achieve your objectives.
- Guidance for the trustees on how to record future decisions in the trust's minute book, that is, guidance on the wording of the minutes they should be making.

✻ Practical ongoing trust administration seminars to assist the trustees when they have queries relating to the trust.

My clients are supplied with draft minutes covering all usual decisions such as the purchase and sale of assets, the making of loans and loan repayments, payments to beneficiaries and end of year minutes.

For an advisor's advice to be of any use they must have established a trust themselves, and have practical experience in the running of trusts, so they can also give the trustees practical running instructions and ongoing assistance with the administration of the trust.

WHY TRUSTEES NEED ACCESS TO ADMINISTRATION SEMINARS

Everything new is strange to start with, and appears to be difficult. In my experience, the monthly asset protection planning administration seminars which my company runs for its clients, have proved invaluable in assisting them to overcome the mental barriers which prevent them from realising that administration is simple. The reason our seminars are run for clients only is that they are designed to assist clients in filling out the draft minutes contained in the minute book of the indexed and tabbed asset protection planning folders they receive as part of their asset protection plan. We also help them to better use the comprehensive notes for guidance on the administration of the trust which are given to them. The seminars also resolve day-to-day practical issues and give clients the knowledge to keep records simply.[6]

TRUSTEES NEED TRUST REVIEWS

Not only does an asset protection plan need to be tailor-made to ensure that it will achieve your objectives, but it needs to be updated as law and circumstances change. In addition to reviewing the asset protection plan yourself, you must seek periodic reviews by experts. By implementing and regularly reviewing an asset protection plan, you will die knowing that you have left your partner or other loved ones a well thought out and executed plan which is current and understood by all.[7]

SUMMARY

→ It is not sensible to prepare an asset protection plan without operating instructions, and without a programme for its future maintenance.

→ The Achilles heel of many trusts is that while care is taken in the drafting of the trust deed and the transfer of assets to the trust, many advisors unwisely take a hands-off approach to the subsequent administration of the trust.

→ Insist on an expert preparing your comprehensive asset protection plan, and ensure that it includes detailed and practical running instructions and draft minutes.

10

WHAT IS
A TRUST?

*If a man dies and leaves his estate
in an uncertain condition, the
lawyers become his heirs.*

EDGAR WATSON HOWE

WHAT IS A TRUST?

A trust (also known as a 'family trust') is similar to a living will. The only major difference is that it works while you are alive, and you can be the trustee or trustees. It is just a legal document containing rules that the trustees have to follow for the running of the trust — just like a company constitution, or the rules of an incorporated society. In effect, a trust acts as a buffer between you and third parties. It is not complicated to set up. It can be modern and user-friendly. The following best sum up what a trust is.

> *The trust is one of the most important and flexible institutions of modern English law. For the management of property which is not in the hands of a sole adult owner, it is rivalled only by the limited liability company.*[1]

> *A trust is an equitable obligation binding a person (who is called a trustee) to deal with property over which he has control (which is called trust property), for the benefit of persons (who are called beneficiaries . . .), of whom he may himself be one and any one of whom may enforce the obligation.*[2]

The term 'trust' refers to the legal relationships created by a person, the settlor, when assets have been placed under the control of a trustee for the benefit of a beneficiary or beneficiaries. A trust has the following characteristics:

❋ The assets of the trust are a separate fund and are not part of the trustee's own assets.

❋ Title to the trust assets is in the name of the trustee or in the name of another person on behalf of the trustee.

❋ The trustee has the power and the duty, in respect of which he/she is accountable, to manage, employ or dispose of the assets in accordance with the terms of the trust and the special duties imposed upon him/her by law.

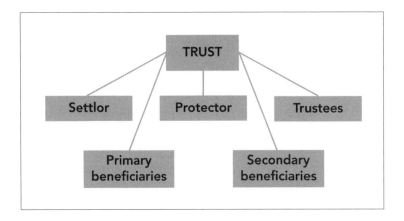

THE SETTLOR

In New Zealand, the 'real' settlors should always be named as the settlors. The person setting up the trust is called the settlor. The settlor's role depends on the terms of the trust deed. Trust deeds vary considerably. In my own trust deeds, the settlor simply sets up the trust and has no other important powers. The important powers are held by the trustees and the protector. In other trust deeds, the settlor is given important powers. You cannot generalise about trusts or the terms used in them.

Unless taxation laws require otherwise, a third party should never be named as a settlor. As in all other areas of trust law, copying what others have done for years without inquiry is unwise. For generations it has been usual in New Zealand to name a third party as a settlor. The fact that others have done so in the past provides no justification for continuing to do so in future.

In cases where 'dummy' settlors are named in trust deeds, they normally have no powers or future role. To pretend to exclude them from future benefits (which they were never going to receive in any event) is a pretence that has no legal benefit. Invariably, such dummy settlors do not, and never intend to, settle assets on the trust. As a matter of common sense, pretences of this nature can only damage credibility and should not be used unless taxation laws necessitate them.

For the purposes of New Zealand income tax, section OB1 of the Income Tax Act 1994 (New Zealand) says that the real settlor is the settlor for income tax purposes.

In Australia a third party settlor may afford taxation benefits. The effect of section 102 of the Income Tax Assessment Act 1936 is that where a person declares that they hold property on trust, and that person may themselves be or become a beneficiary of the trust, the Commissioner may treat the trust as the 'alter ego' of the trustee and subject that person to tax on all of the trust income. In Australia it is common to avoid this problem by having an independent settlor, and providing in the trust deed that the settlor can receive no benefits from the trust.[3] In one case, one of the beneficiaries settled further monies on a trustee. Strangely, the court held that section 102 could not be applied, drawing a distinction between the creation of the trust and the settlement of further funds on an existing trust.

THE TRUSTEES

The trustees of a trust are the people who make the decisions (just like the trustees of a will).[4] They make sure the rules set out in the trust deed are followed. A trustee is similar to a director of a company. There is no statutory restriction preventing the appointment of a sole trustee in the trust deed. You can be the only trustee of the trust. Legally, there is not, and never has been, a need to appoint 'independent' trustees. A trust with the settlor as the sole trustee or one of the trustees is legally valid, as long as the settlor is not the sole beneficiary.[5] The Privy Council (New Zealand's highest court) has also accepted that a trust is valid where the settlor is the sole trustee and one of a number of beneficiaries.[6] Who the trustees should be depends on your wishes and objectives.

Trustee companies will act as independent trustees, as will some lawyers and accountants. If you decide to appoint an independent trustee, in my opinion you must also appoint a protector with power to remove the trustees. A trust without power to remove trustees is not desirable.

Past court cases have established that far more trusts with independent trustees have been set aside as invalid, or 'shams', than trusts without independent trustees. This occurs because advisors rarely advise trustees of their legal responsibilities, and the requirements that must be satisfied for decisions of trustees to be valid. Such independent trustees are rarely, in fact, independent. They are often selected because advisors have told the settlor that independent trustees are necessary. In practice, they often act as 'rubber stamps' who are not consulted (or at least not genuinely consulted) before decisions are made concerning the trust. If that happens, the decisions are 'sham' transactions and invalid. If that occurs frequently enough, it provides evidence that there was never any intention to create a trust. The trust may therefore be declared invalid and a 'sham'.

This has occurred in many cases because of the failure, in practice, of many independent trustees to realise the need to genuinely take part in decisions involving the trust. It has also occurred due to failure on the part of the 'client' trustees to understand what a trust is, and how to exercise the duties of trustees. The case of Mr G. and Miss P. illustrates the disasters that might occur through the failure of the independent trustee to act genuinely.

Mr F., a partner in a law firm, established trusts for a couple, Mr G. and Miss P., in 1994. When I reviewed the trust, Mr G. stated that , 'Mr F. told me that I should be the settlor of the trust which I set up. He told me that it was essential that he be a trustee along with me.' Miss P. was settlor of the trust set up by her, with the trustees being Miss P. and Mr F. 'We sold our house to the two trusts (subject to an occupation lease in our favour), at the then three-year-old government valuation in order to keep the sale price down. Mr F. did not view the property, or make any inquiries about it.' In effect, Mr F. rubber stamped the purchase by the trusts. These transactions were accordingly invalid.

'We were given no guidance by Mr F. on our obligations as trustees, and did not realise the need to involve him in future decisions of the trusts.' Miss P. and Mr G. heard nothing about the trusts from Mr F. for the next five years. 'We purchased substantial investments in the names of both trusts over the next five years. We did not tell Mr F.' As a result, all of these investment decisions were invalid. No gifting was carried out during that period, and the trust deeds and trust records were not reviewed by Mr F.

It is essential that all independent trustees should exercise their functions in a proper manner and not as a nominee or agent for the settlors.

How old does a trustee have to be?

In New Zealand, Australia and Britain there are no legislative provisions preventing any otherwise competent natural trustee from being appointed as an original trustee of a trust. Trustees who are natural persons must have the legal capacity to hold title to property, and must have the mental capacity to do so.

In New South Wales it is provided that a person under the age of 18 may not be a trustee.[7]

How trustees should make valid decisions

When making a decision as to who the trustees should be, it must be remembered that the trustees are required (amongst other things) to observe and maintain the following basic legal requirements (which are dealt with in detail in my book *Asset Protection Planning, Trusts and the Administration of Trusts*):

✤ To keep full records of all decisions made. It becomes easier to examine a decision if the reasons for it have been disclosed.[8]

✤ To act honestly and in good faith. Trustees must act honestly and in good faith in relation to the trust property for the benefit of the beneficiaries.[9]

✤ To ensure that all trustees take part in all decisions unless otherwise permitted by statute or the terms of the trust deed. If they do not the decision will be invalid.

> *Trustees must act in good faith, responsibly and reasonably. They must inform themselves, before making a decision, of matters which are relevant to the decision. These matters may not be limited to simple matters of fact but will, on occasion (indeed, quite often) include taking advice from appropriate experts, whether the experts are lawyers, accountants, actuaries, surveyors, scientists or whomsoever. It is, however, for advisors to advise and for trustees to decide: trustees may not (except in so far as they are authorised to do so) delegate the exercise of their discretions, even to experts.*[10]

✤ To consider whether their discretion should be exercised. If the trustees (or any one of them) fail altogether to exercise the duties of consideration, the court can set aside the purported exercise of their discretion, if satisfied that the trustees never exercised the power. The trustees' decision in that event will be a nullity.[11]

✗ To observe the terms of the trust deed. Failure to carry out the terms of the trust deed, so long as its requirements are legal, is a breach of trust.[12]

✗ To treat all beneficiaries fairly and impartially. Trustees must put aside personal interests and consider the overall interests of all beneficiaries.[13]

In my experience these fundamental trustee obligations are not brought to the attention of, and are therefore rarely observed in practice by, independent trustees.

THE BENEFICIARIES

The beneficiaries are the people entitled to the assets of the trust. Most well prepared trusts are discretionary trusts. What that means is that none of the beneficiaries is entitled to anything unless the trustees say so at their discretion. The beneficiaries of a discretionary trust, who are not takers in default of appointment (that is, the beneficiaries entitled to receive the trust fund at the end of the period of the trust, if the trustees do not distribute the trust fund to other beneficiaries prior to that date) do not have any right to the trust assets, but they have a right to be considered as potential recipients of benefits by the trustees and a right to have their interests protected by a court of equity.[14]

There should be two classes of beneficiaries. Firstly, primary beneficiaries. These beneficiaries are to benefit both while you are alive and after your death. These will often include your children, other close blood relatives and, in some cases, charities. In other words, yourself and the people currently named as beneficiaries in your will. Secondary beneficiaries are 'backstop' beneficiaries, that is, they are the beneficiaries who inherit if all of your primary beneficiaries die.

THE PROTECTOR

The protector is normally the dispute resolver. While the appointment of a protector is common in trusts created in offshore financial centres, most New Zealand trust deeds contain no such protector provisions. The protector's functions (which vary from trust to trust) normally include the following:

❋ To appoint and remove trustees.

❋ To resolve disputes between trustees (to avoid the need to refer the dispute to the High Court).

❋ Following the death or mental incapacity of the settlor, as a matter of common sense and in order to limit the possibility of any disputes between trustees and/or beneficiaries and/or between trustees and beneficiaries (while recognising that the final decision on such matters rests with the trustees), to:

— distribute copies of the then current Memorandum of Wishes of the settlor of the trust to the trustees,

— hold a meeting with the trustees in order to advise them of the wishes of the settlor as expressed in such Memorandum of Wishes, and to ascertain whether there are any potential differences of opinion between the trustees,

— use the powers given to him, her or them to resolve any such differences,

— convene a meeting of the trustees and the beneficiaries of the trust in order to advise such beneficiaries of the wishes of the settlor as expressed in such Memorandum of Wishes; advise them that the Memorandum of Wishes is not legally binding on the trustees; enable the trustees to explain to the beneficiaries their current intentions in relation to the assets and income of the trust fund; explain to such beneficiaries the benefits of having a trust established for their own benefit and the wishes (if any) expressed in the settlor's Memorandum of Wishes as to the resettlement of capital payments to such beneficiaries' trusts; ascertain whether there are any potential differences of opinion between the trustees and such beneficiaries; and assist in the resolution of any such differences.

You will normally be the protector. After your mental disability or death the protector should normally be someone with no axe to grind, someone who is not a trustee or beneficiary of the trust, as they will be the ones involved in any dispute which arises, and someone who is familiar with your objectives.

There have been very few decisions on the role of the protector, and most of the decisions have been made in the offshore financial centres. In a number of these centres, the role of the protector has been provided for by legislation, and the decisions in those jurisdictions are accordingly of limited use.

What has been lost sight of by some is that a number of the powers given by trust deeds to protectors have in the past been given to settlors and appointors. Accordingly, there are precedents on the manner in which some of the powers given to a protector are likely to be dealt with by a court.

To avoid doubts as to what duties the protector owes to the beneficiaries, the trust deed should provide that the protector must act honestly and in good faith for the benefit of the primary beneficiaries during their lifetime, and for the benefit of the secondary beneficiaries after the death of the primary beneficiaries.

PROVISIONS THAT MUST BE INCLUDED IN TRUST DEEDS

Your circumstances, the circumstances of your loved ones and the law will change. The trust must be flexible enough to cope with such changes. For this reason, the trust deed should include the following provisions:

Power to alter the Family Trust Deed

There is no reason why the trust deed cannot include a power of variation.[15] The trust deed must include power for the trustees to alter the trust deed. This is essential to enable the trust deed to be changed as your circumstances, the law and Inland Revenue Department rulings change, or if court decisions clarify the law. A trust without such a clause is not only a white elephant, but is extremely dangerous. For example, in March 1996 the New Zealand Inland Revenue Department issued a binding ruling concerning, among other things, the taxation treatment of gifts made to trusts. As a result, if the primary beneficiaries of the trust included companies or other non-natural entities (other than charities), taxation liability (not gift duty) is payable on the amount of the gift. The trust deeds I work with were modified after that ruling to make them safe in that regard, as well as to incorporate other improvements. If you have a trust without such a clause, my recommendation is that you do not put any more assets into that trust, and change your advisor if he/she has not advised you of the need to restructure.

Power of resettlement

The trust deed should also include power to resettle (transfer) the trust property to another trust in which one of the beneficiaries is also a beneficiary. These clauses (which are common in trusts) are essential to enable restructuring from a single trust to mirror trusts or a new trust, and to enable the assets which the beneficiaries receive from the trust to be paid directly to a trust set up for the benefit of that beneficiary (even if they set it up at that time) without gifting or gift duty.

Portability provisions

The trust should include portability provisions. These enable the trustees to change the jurisdiction of the trust, alter the laws that apply to it, and generally to take it wherever the trustees go. It can also be used to purchase property in other countries. Many of my clients have benefited from the inclusion of these clauses, which are still rare in New Zealand trusts. None of us know where our children or grandchildren will end up.

The power to add additional beneficiaries

It has been established that discretionary trusts[16] can contain wide powers to add or subtract beneficiaries. Taxation laws may result in the need to have a narrower power to add additional beneficiaries (as is the case in New Zealand). You should always record your reasons for exercising that power in writing in the minute book.

SUCCESS THROUGH RUNNING
THE TRUST HONESTLY[17]

It is a frequently overlooked fact that trusts must be administered with credibility and genuineness. In *Potter and Monroe's Tax Planning with Precedents*[18] the authors warned, in words which are as true today as when they were first written, that 'A man cannot eat his cake and have it. Moreover, it is not the function of his lawyer to devise a scheme whereby this fact of life is falsified. If a man disposes of his property for another's benefit, certain tax results may follow; but the results cannot be achieved unless the disposition is in the first place effected not as a fiction but as a fact.'

Credibility is created by acting genuinely, not by pretending to do so. Creditable asset protection plans are also created by acting genuinely, and not pretending to do so. Previous cases have established that even if you set up a trust, if you, in your personal capacity, intend to keep complete control over and power to deal with the property transferred to the trust, the court will say that there is no trust.

The cases which have been set aside on these grounds have one common factor — a lack of a genuine intention to create a trust. If the parties had acted genuinely the trusts or transactions would not have been shams.

The consequences of a sham (pretend) trust are disastrous. Every payment to beneficiaries out of the trust must be repaid by the trustees to the settlor, and the settlor must be placed back in the same position as he/she would have been if the trust had not been established (whether or not the loss was foreseeable). Any limitation of liability clauses in a sham trust perish with the sham trust.

Once it is determined that the trust is a sham, its assets are held in a resulting trust for the settlor. The invalidity cannot be cured. If this occurs, and if the settlor is able and willing to do so, a new trust will need to be established, and the assets sold by the settlor at their then current market value to the new trust. This will not be possible if the settlor is deceased, bankrupt or incapacitated. The subject of sham trusts is dealt with in the book *Sham Trusts*.

WHAT TYPE OF TRUST DO YOU NEED?

The type of trust you need will often be determined by the taxation and estate duty laws of your country or state. Trust deeds in New Zealand, Australia, Hong Kong, most tax havens and the United

Kingdom are very similar. On the other hand, trust deeds in the United States are prepared in a completely different manner for estate duty avoidance reasons. If estate duty is abolished, however, the drafting of trusts in the United States could change significantly. You need to take expert advice about provisions needed in your trust deed as a result of the taxation and estate duty laws in your country.

TYPES OF TRUSTS

Single trusts

Most trusts are single trusts with the features shown on page 93. Your age, the value of your assets, and your objectives are the major factors for consideration as to the type of trust appropriate for you.

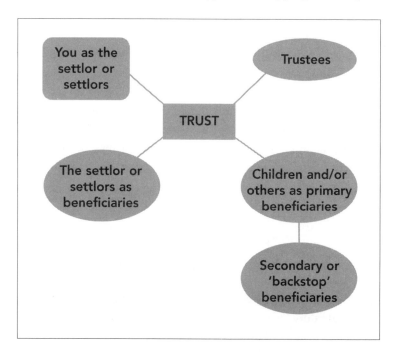

You normally do not need to set up cross/mirror trusts if there is no possibility of future estate duty in your case, or you do not wish to benefit from the trust. In such cases one modern flexible trust is often all you need, whether you are single or part of a couple.

Cross/mirror trusts

The major difference between single trusts and cross/mirror trusts is that in the case of cross/mirror trusts the settlor is not a beneficiary of the trust established by him/her (being the trust to which his/her assets are sold). As a result (oversimplifying the position), the settlor cannot benefit from the assets sold by him/her to that trust.

The main reason for the use of cross/mirror trusts is to remove the risk that the assets transferred to the trust will be treated as assets in his/her estate, for estate duty purposes only.

The need for cross/mirror trusts to avoid estate duty in New Zealand and the United Kingdom

Prior to the abolition of estate duty in New Zealand in 1992, most advisors prepared cross/mirror trusts for clients with potential estate duty problems in order to help them avoid those problems. The cross/mirror trust structure is the only one which is capable of avoiding estate duty liability. Put simply, there are no other options which are capable of doing this, and no one has suggested that there are.

The safest view is that a settlor needs cross/mirror trusts if he/she would otherwise have to pay estate duty or inheritance tax and the settlor does not want to be excluded as a beneficiary of his or her partner's trust.

I believe that those establishing single trusts in New Zealand for settlors who are potential estate duty or inheritance tax candidates, could be liable for substantial damages in the event of estate duty returning, especially if they fail to advise the settlor of the possibility of its reintroduction and the potential problems that new estate duty laws may cause for the settlor.

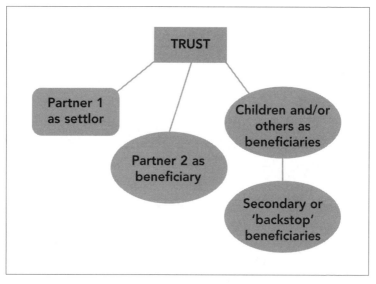

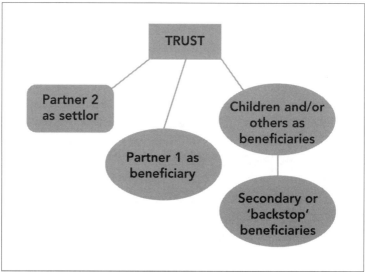

Parallel trusts

In New Zealand, a number of lawyers recommend parallel trusts for settlors with potential estate duty liability. Parallel trusts are simply rebadged cross/mirror trusts, with both of the settlors

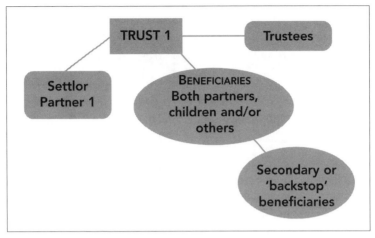

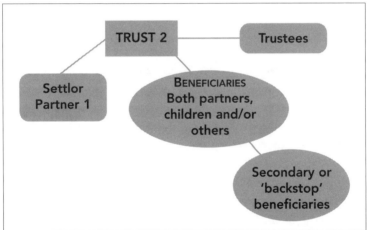

being beneficiaries of both of the trusts. What is frequently overlooked is that parallel trusts will still suffer from the same deficiencies that their proponents maintain cross/mirror trusts suffer from in the event of estate duty being reintroduced. In that event, the settlor will be deleted as a beneficiary of the trust established by him/her for estate duty reasons.

In my view, the logic of those advocating parallel trusts is dangerous, and in many cases parallel trusts are unnecessary, for the following reasons:

✳ You will be lending further amounts to the trusts and are unlikely to need to receive funds from the trusts until after your retirement. Accordingly, cross/mirror trusts will not disadvantage you during your working life. The trusts can be amended later as required.

✳ If you do not presently need to benefit from the trust, it is difficult to understand why you should take such unnecessary risks without any corresponding benefit. Few of us know when we are going to die. None of us know whether we will live for three or seven years after estate duty is reintroduced, or whether there will be time for the removal of the settlor as a beneficiary so that the trust is able to become effective for estate duty purposes if estate duty is reintroduced. This is a matter of logic, not law.

With any modern trust, the trustees can, if appropriate, add and remove beneficiaries to and from the trust. Such powers exist to enable the trusts to be changed if the law, its interpretation, or circumstances change. Accordingly, in the event of a settlor with an estate duty problem needing to be added as a beneficiary of a trust, it will be legally possible for the trustees, so long as they are acting honestly and in good faith, to do so at that time. A review of the legal consequences of such additions (such as potential estate duty liability) can be made at the time of the addition in the light of the law as it is then.

No one can predict the form in which estate duty will be reintroduced. However, for the reasons detailed below and planning for the worst, if estate duty is reintroduced in the form in which it previously existed in New Zealand, Australia, Canada, and as it currently stands in England, a settlor will be liable for estate duty for a period of three years (seven in England) after he/she is removed as a beneficiary of the trust.

It is unwise to assume, as the proponents of parallel trusts do, that some new untried form of estate duty will be introduced.

SUCCESS THROUGH MAKING SURE
THE TRUST IS SIMPLE TO RUN

Why amnesia is the answer

Most difficulties arise simply because you think that running a trust
will be hard. It won't be if you have running instructions. After all,
you are simply making the same investment decisions as before, but
in your new capacity — as trustee of the trust. If anything, it is
easier than before. You just get a great new filing system with easy
to follow instructions on how to keep the investment records.

As the trust's bank account is used only for trust investments,
trust asset sales and trust income, all investment information is now
on the one set of bank statements. It is no longer muddled in with
your personal expenditure on your personal bank statements. By
simplifying your affairs in this way before you die, you will substantially reduce estate administration costs.

Amnesia is the best solution. Forget everything you have been
told about trusts. Think it will be easy to run and it will be (so long
as you have the notes for guidance). If you think it is going to be
hard, it will be. In other words, think and act positively for success.

THE TRUST INVESTS

Because the trust invests and you spend in order to achieve
personal poverty, you must never use the trust's bank account for
your personal income and expenditure. The trust invests, and you
spend. Keep it that simple, and it will stay that simple. The moment
you break the rule, not only have you made something simple
difficult, but you have damaged the credibility of the trust by
treating the trust's bank account as if it was still yours.

YOU SPEND

Through your spending you get poor. Your personal income still goes into your personal bank account, which continues to be used for your personal expenditure, just as before. The only change is that your personal bank account is kept completely separate from that of the trust.

SUMMARY

→ A trust is like a living will.

→ Many problems with trusts are caused by a lack of knowledge on the part of the advisors founding the trust. In some cases they fail to understand the basic trust law requirements for the creation and administration of a valid trust, and in others they fail to provide trustees with practical guidance on what is legally required to administer the trust thereafter.

→ It is essential that all trustees genuinely take part in the decisions of trustees, and that detailed records of trustees' decisions are kept, in order to avoid sham trusts and sham trust transactions.

→ Put aside any thoughts that the trust will be difficult to run.

→ So long as you have detailed running instructions, a trust can be simpler to run than your own affairs were previously.

→ Keep it simple. You spend using your own bank account. The trust invests using its bank account.[19]

11

SUCCESS THROUGH MAKING SURE YOUR ASSET PROTECTION PLAN WORKS

We may stop ourselves when going up,
never when going down.

NAPOLEON BONAPARTE

SUCCESS THROUGH FUTURE INCREASES IN THE VALUE OF ASSETS BELONGING TO THE TRUST

As previously detailed, personal poverty and a rich trust are now your objectives. However, many people with trusts use them as band-aids and not as solutions. They will not succeed as well as those with a trust that is part of an asset protection plan.

Remember the case of Bill and Joy (see chapter 3)? They started their asset protection plan in 1990. They only sold their family home to the trust because their lawyer said there was no point in selling their company to the trust until the first lot of gifting was finished. Their company was then worth $200,000 but, 'over the next five years the company's business expanded, and we saved $500,000 from the company's profits. By 1995, the company was worth $500,000 as a result of the increase in its profitability. We now realise that we should have sold everything to the trust at once. What would have taken us four years to gift at a value of $200,000 will now take us twenty years to gift.' This is sixteen years longer than if everything had been sold to the trust at the same time in 1990. They now regret not having their asset protection plan prepared by an expert. As Bill and Joy are now aware, you cannot achieve your objective of personal poverty and a rich trust if you are getting wealthier as a result of personal savings out of private company or investment income.

If you and the trust invest, what are you trying to achieve? If this is what you are doing, the short answer is that your trust is not part of a well thought out asset protection plan. If you are making yourself and the trust rich, you are also making your life unnecessarily complicated by duplicating records, taxation returns and bank accounts required for investments.

You can only achieve personal poverty and a rich trust through the trust investing and you spending.

SUCCESS THROUGH THE TRUST
INHERITING WEALTH

If you inherit wealth, you do so regardless of your circumstances. If the trust established for your benefit inherits wealth from loved ones, it is never yours and cannot be taken from you. The trustees of the trust can use their common sense in the special circumstances that occur from time to time.

As part of your asset protection plan, your will should be changed to leave all assets not already in the trust to the trust on your death. The function of your will is simply to conclude any gifting not completed by you at the time of your death, and to put into the trust all assets still owned by you personally.

In the case of loved ones, if their assets are not all in a trust you simply need to persuade them to change their wills to leave your inheritance to the trust instead of to you personally. Your loved ones do not have to understand trusts, only that by leaving the inheritance to the trust it will not go to the government or to others.

If your loved ones have all of their assets in trusts, all decent trusts contain a provision permitting assets to be transferred to a trust formed for the benefit of that beneficiary (and others). As long as the strategy of personal poverty and a rich trust are followed, your asset protection plan will work.

SUCCESS THROUGH YOUR LOVED
ONES INHERITING TRUSTS

In the case of your loved ones, they should inherit trusts and not assets. The assets are then one hundred percent safe.

In the case of William and Samantha (see chapter 3), following their deaths their two daughters will each inherit a trust with 50 percent of the assets in it. The daughters will then become the sole trustee of one of the trusts each at age 25. They will be able to invest the assets in their capacity as trustee, in just the same manner as they would have invested the funds if they had inherited them personally. As beneficiaries they can be paid both capital and income from the trust, at the discretion of the trustee. The trustee needs to act honestly and in good faith. The beneficiary will only need funds from the trust if there is not enough in their personal bank account to cover their personal expenditure. They do not need funds for investment as the trust invests. They only spend.

Some people setting up trusts wish the assets to remain in the trusts for the long-term benefit of their loved ones. They may want the income to be used for the benefit of their loved ones, and most of the capital to be kept intact and invested in growth investments for the benefit of future generations. In such cases, the trustees may be authorised to purchase residences for the use of beneficiaries.

The asset protection plan must be tailor made to achieve your important objectives. Whatever your objectives are, through a trust you are allowing your trustees to use their common sense in circumstances which you cannot predict, rather than your will forcing the trustees to pay out to beneficiaries regardless of their personal circumstances.

SUMMARY

→ If you and the trust are investing, you cannot achieve personal poverty and a rich trust. That is only possible through the trust investing and you spending. If you inherit wealth, you do so regardless of your circumstances, often later in life. If the trust established for your benefit inherits wealth from loved ones, it is never yours and cannot be taken from you.

✦ In the case of your loved ones, they should inherit trusts and not assets. The assets are then one hundred percent safe. Through a trust, you are allowing your trustees to use their common sense in circumstances that you cannot predict.[1]

12

SUCCESS THROUGH GETTING POOR ASAP

Luck is the residue of design.

BRANCH RICKEY

SUCCESS THROUGH GETTING POORER
BY GIFTING TO THE TRUST

The object of all good asset protection planning is for you to get poor as soon as possible, and to do this as far as possible in advance of any potential problems.

Step one is the sale of your assets to the trust. You need to get advice on the capital gains tax and other taxation consequences which the sale of the assets will cause, as these vary from country to country.

As a result of the sale of the assets to the trust, the trust gives you back an IOU (a Deed of Acknowledgment of Debt).

Step two involves gifting that IOU to the trust to make you personally poor and the trust rich. Gifting is simply saying to the trust, 'Do not pay me back.' It is done on paper by a deed.

Gift duty

In countries where there is no gift duty, all assets can be gifted to the trust at once. In countries that impose gift duty on the gifting of assets above certain values, the assets can be sold to the trust in exchange for an IOU or Deed of Acknowledgment of Debt. The Deed of Acknowledgment of Debt is then gifted progressively. In New Zealand you can gift $27,000 per person per year in total.

In New Zealand gift duty is payable where the value of the gift and any other gifts made by the maker within the twelve-month period exceeds $27,000. Gift duty is imposed at the following rates in New Zealand:

$	%	$	%
1–27,000	Nil	27,001–36,000	5
36,001–54,000	10	54,001–72,000	20
72,001 and higher	25		

In New Zealand, it is normal to annually gift $27,000 of the loan owed to you by the trust to the trust. This reduces the debt owed by the trust to you. For instance, if the trust owes you $500,000, you would on the date of the sale, say 1 October 2000, gift the trust $27,000. The trust then owes you $473,000. Future gifts would be made annually on the anniversary of the date of the first gift. So, on 1 October 2001 you would gift the trust a further $27,000, reducing the debt owed to you by the trust to $446,000, and so on each year until the trust owes you nothing. Remember, your objective is personal poverty and a rich trust. If the next gift is made one day earlier you will be liable for gift duty, and if the gift statement is filed more than three months after the last gift a substantial penalty can be imposed.

Exemptions from gift duty in New Zealand

Small gifts
Section 71 of the Estate and Gift Duties Act 1968 (New Zealand) exempts small gifts where the total value of gifts made by the same giver to the same receiver in the same calendar year does not exceed $2000. Inland Revenue has to be satisfied that the gifts are made in good faith as part of the normal expenditure of the giver. A gift is made in good faith if there is no intention to avoid payment of New Zealand tax or duty by means of the gift.

What constitutes normal expenditure will depend on the gift-maker's circumstances. Inland Revenue considers that normal expenditure is that which any person of similar social or religious background could reasonably incur. It need not be normal in the more restricted sense of being recurring, habitual or regular.

Small gifts, such as $10 or $100 amounts that a settlor uses to create a trust, are considered normal expenditure. However, Inland

Revenue do not regard continually making small gifts to an already established trust as being in good faith.

Gifts for maintenance or education of relatives

Section 72 of the Estate and Gift Duties Act 1968 (New Zealand) exempts gifts made for the maintenance or education of relatives. Inland Revenue has to be satisfied that the gift is not excessive in amount, having regard to the legal or moral obligation of the gift-maker to provide maintenance or means of education.[1] Each particular gift and its surrounding circumstances is considered when deciding whether Section 72 applies.

HOW GIFTING MUST BE CARRIED OUT

The manner in which gifting must be carried out is a matter of common law or of other statute law. Normally, the gift is made by a deed called a Deed of Forgiveness of Debt. Do not look for the logic (as there is not much logic in the law). A deed is needed to make the gift legally valid because no amount has been paid in exchange for the gift. If not the gift is void.[2] To be valid the law requires that all deeds must be witnessed by another person.[3]

Always take legal advice on how the Deed of Forgiveness of Debt is worded. In New Zealand, you must include the wording 'in consideration of natural love and affection' in the deed of forgiveness of debt. If you do not then income tax may be payable on the gift under the Income Tax Act (New Zealand) accruals rules. Deeds of Forgiveness of Debt cannot be backdated. They are not effective until the deed is executed.[4]

In New Zealand, in addition to completing the Deed of Forgiveness of Debt, two originals of the gift statements (form IR 196) and one photocopy (not original) of the Deed of Forgiveness of Debt must be received by the Inland Revenue Department in

Christchurch[5] within three months of the date of the gift. The gift statement does not legally make a gift. The Deed of Forgiveness of Debt legally makes the gift.

OCCUPATION LEASES

Note: You do not need to read this section unless you are rich and live in a country which imposes gift duty (which therefore prevents you from gifting everything at once to the trust) and that permits you to enter into a lease with yourself (as is the case in New Zealand).

If you are rich, an occupation lease is one of the few ways of getting poorer more quickly. You should only consider an occupation lease when you cannot reduce the value of your assets fast enough through normal gifting. You do not need an occupation lease if a normal gifting programme will result in your trust owning all your assets prior to the time you are likely to enter long term geriatric care or die. An occupation lease is either the grant to yourself of a lease for a term of years over your property, or the grant to yourself of a lease for your lifetime over your property. In both cases it permits you to live in your home for the term you continue to pay all of the outgoings. In New Zealand you can grant an occupation lease over your property to yourself as it is accepted in practice by the Inland Revenue Department.[6]

The benefit of an occupation lease is that it reduces the value of your interest in the property. This is because you keep the value of living in the house for your life. The trust gets no income or other benefit until you die. The lease has no value after the death of you as lessee (tenant).

The reduction in the value of your interest in the property will be of importance if there might otherwise be estate duty liability on your death. When deciding whether or not you need an occupation lease the following factors need to be taken into account.

Normal gifting totally removes the value of the property from your assets. An occupation lease does not. Until your death, or the death of the second partner in the case of a couple, the occupation lease has a value. An occupation lease makes the interest in the property being purchased by your trust worth a lot less, without gifting. The younger you are, the greater the reduction. When your occupation lease comes to an end on your death, the right to the possession of the property belongs to the current lessor (owner) of the property (the trust).

If you are planning to sell your property in the not too distant future, the legal costs of the occupation lease must be considered. Legal costs will be payable on creation of the occupation lease and on discharge of the occupation lease when you sell the property. The new home must be purchased in your name, a new occupation lease registered over the replacement property, and the replacement property must then be transferred to the trust a short time later, subject to the occupation lease. You may decide that cost factors mean it is better to wait until you have sold the property and repurchased.

In New Zealand, the interest created by the occupation lease has a value, being the present value of income on capital of $1.00 for life as set out in Table A or B (see Appendix) of the Second Schedule to the Estate and Gift Duties Act 1968 (New Zealand), multiplied by the current market value of your property.

The value of the occupation lease can only be calculated on the basis of Table A or B of the Second Schedule if you do not know of any health problems which may shorten your life expectancy. If you are a couple and only one of you has no health problems that may shorten your life expectancy, then the value of the occupation lease can be calculated in accordance with that person's life expectancy as set out in Table A or B. If both of you have health problems that may shorten your life expectancy, then an actuarial valuation of the value of your occupation lease must be obtained.

Referring to Table A or B, work out the value of the occupation lease of your own home using the following steps.

If there are two of you, look at the life expectancy of the younger of you and compare that with the life expectancy of the older. The life expectancy can be found in the second column of that table.

Using the Table A or B figures for the one with the longest life expectancy, look at the last column for your age which sets out the present value of income on capital of $1.00 for life. Multiply that figure by the current market value of your property. This gives the value of the occupation lease which you are creating for the property.

You also need to be aware that an occupation lease substantially increases as a result of inflation at an assumed rate of 4 percent for a substantial number of years after its creation, as shown in the following chart .[7]

Future value of a lease for life with property values increasing at 4% p.a. (all in thousands of dollars)

Year	Property value	Age at entry			
		30	40	50	60
1	300	174	159	137	109
5	244	204	182	151	114
10	298	237	205	163	115
15	364	272	226	170	112
20	445	306	243	172	105
30	663	362	257	157	79
40	988	382	234	117	49
50	1473	349	175	73	
60	2195	261	109		
70	3273	163			

In New Zealand, the Inland Revenue Department in their binding ruling on Section 70(2) of the Estate and Gift Duties Act,[8] stated that it is not necessary to register the occupation lease under the Land Transfer Act 1952. I recommend that for safety, the occupation lease be registered.

The procedure to be followed when creating an occupation lease

In New Zealand, the Inland Revenue Department's view[9] is that there is no gift duty liability if, when creating an occupation lease for your existing property, you first create a life estate, or lease for a term of years, over the property, then transfer the remainder (reversionary) interest in the property to the trust. The remainder interest is what is left of the property after creation of the occupation lease.

If this procedure is not followed, and you transfer your existing property to the trust at the same time as you create the occupation lease, then in New Zealand you will be caught for gift duty by Section 70(2) of the Estate and Gift Duties Act (New Zealand).

In New Zealand, no tax is payable[10] on granting an occupation lease, so long as you create the occupation lease first in favour of yourself, and later enter into the occupation lease.[11]

What happens when you sell a property which has an occupation lease and purchase a replacement property with an occupation lease?

Your occupation lease should include a clause allowing the sale of the property with the consent of you as the tenant and the trust as the lessor (landlord) and lessee (tenant), on the basis that a replacement property is purchased by you as the lessee as to the 'occupation lease interest' on the same terms as the existing lease, and by the trust as the lessor as to the remainder interest.

The reason for this clause is to enable the ready sale of the property, and the purchase of a replacement property.

In order to sell the property when it is subject to an occupation lease you must surrender that lease. To surrender the lease you need to sign a surrender of lease document, a procedure that is no more complicated than discharging a mortgage. You then need to do the following:

- ✳ Calculate the additional amount owed to you by the trust as a result of the surrender of the occupation lease.

- ✳ Take a new occupation lease on the replacement house and then, after a month or so, sell that house to the trust subject to the occupation lease.

- ✳ Calculate the amount owed by the trust to you as a result of the purchase of the replacement house subject to the occupation lease.

The reasons for this are:

As detailed above, your occupation lease has a value determined in accordance with Table A or B (see Appendix) of the Second Schedule to the Estate and Gift Duties Act 1968. That value does not simply disappear when the occupation lease is first created. The value is reduced in accordance with those tables, as your age increases. At any time, you can determine the value of your occupation lease by multiplying the then current market value of the property by the relevant multiplier from the tables. The occupation lease only reaches the stage of having no value when the lease is at an end. In terms of the occupation lease, this will normally be on your death.

In New Zealand, if you voluntarily surrender your occupation lease before the end of the lease, the effect is that the trust, as the owner of the remainder of the property, will then own the entire property without any occupation lease. Unless the trust purchases the value of the occupation lease from you, this surrender will be a gift in terms of the Estate and Gift Duties Act 1968 (New Zealand),[12] on which you will have to pay gift duty if the amount of the gift, together with any other gifts which you have made within a twelve-month period, exceeds $27,000 per person. The amount of this gift, particularly near the commencement of the lease, could be substantial, and the gift duty could also be substantial.

SUMMARY

→ In order to get poor you need to gift what you are now worth to the trust/s. Gifting is simply a method of saying 'do not pay me back'.

→ In countries in which there is no gift duty, all assets can be gifted to the trust at once.

→ In countries that impose gift duty on the gifting of assets above certain values, the assets can be sold to the trust in exchange for a Deed of Acknowledgment of Debt. The Deed of Acknowledgment of Debt is then progressively gifted.

→ If you are rich and an estate duty candidate living in New Zealand, you may need to consider an occupation lease to knock down the value of your home (and beach home if applicable) for estate duty purposes.

→ In all countries, you need to get advice about the capital gains tax and other taxation consequences that the sale of the assets may cause. These vary from country to country.

13

SUCCESS THROUGH THE TRUST BUYING ASSETS AT TODAY'S VALUES

Depend upon the rabbit's foot if you will, but remember, it didn't work for the rabbit!

R.E. SHAY

Why a trust is the only safe option to protect your assets

Put simply, everything else increases your wealth and exposes your assets to risk. If, for instance, you own shares in a company, as the company goes up in value so does your personal wealth.

You have a choice between a trust as part of an asset protection plan or personal ownership of assets. As you have now learned, personal ownership of assets is the same as crossing your fingers and hoping that unforeseen events do not strip the assets from you.

Assets that it is legally possible for a trust to own

A trust can own any asset that an individual can own unless a statutory provision provides to the contrary.[1]

Which assets should you sell to the trust?

Having identified what assets you own for the benefit of your advisor, you need to set out which of those assets you wish to be transferred to the trust/s. The asset protection questionnaire beginning on page 55 will assist you to do so. The decision as to which assets should be sold to the trust primarily involves a decision as to your personal need for cash in the immediate future, and whether the cost that would be involved in transferring a particular asset to the trust/s (for example, stamp duty, taxation, capital gains tax or GST) outweighs the benefits of transferring that asset to the trust/s.

If you intend to sell the asset now or in the near future, it may be cheaper to subsequently transfer the proceeds of sale to the trust/s. In New Zealand, if you sell a property to a trust with the intention of the trust selling it, any profit on the resale by the trust will be taxable. There is no point in turning what would otherwise be a capital gain into a taxable profit if the sale is performed through the trust. Assets must always be sold to the trust for their current market value to avoid a gift duty or possible income tax liability being created.

Assets which will go up in value

As previously detailed, unless there is a major cost that outweighs the benefits, all assets likely to go up in value should be transferred to the trust/s at once. Doing this will keep the set-up costs down by avoiding the duplication of documents that would otherwise be necessary on later transfers of those assets to the trust/s. It will also peg the value of all your assets now. If some assets are left out of the trust/s and go up in value, you will have even more money to gift to the trust/s.

Assets which will go down in value

You should not normally transfer assets that are likely to go down in value to the trust/s until you have completed the rest of your gifting programme. By that time, such assets will probably have dropped even further in value (resulting in it taking less time to gift their sale value to the trust).

For this reason, you (generally) do not initially sell the contents of your home, motor vehicles or smaller pleasure boats to the trust as they are likely to go down in value, particularly as they get older. You should sell these assets to the trust once you have completed the rest of your gifting.

HOW TO SELL ASSETS TO THE TRUST

All the normal legal documents needed to sell the assets in question to the trust must be signed. The documentation varies from country to country and there are different requirements for different types of assets.

Now for some legal mumbo-jumbo. In all cases, a declaration of trust will be legally effective to transfer the equitable estate (which means that the asset is still registered in your name but the courts will force you to complete the legal transfer to the trust if you fail to do so), but not the legal estate (that is, the trust has full ownership of the asset). For your own safety, it is necessary to transfer the legal estate to the trust as well, as otherwise the trust gets no protection against claims against you personally by others, which could result in the trust losing the asset. It is vital that you:

✴ do everything legally necessary to transfer ownership of those assets from you to the trust;

✴ prepare a declaration of trust stating that the trustees hold those assets in trust for the trust, and no longer own them personally. This will establish that assets previously owned by you are now owned by the trust.

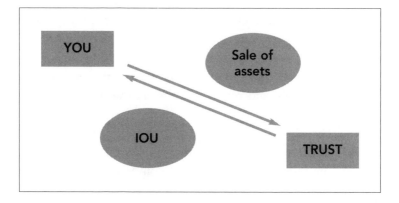

Normally, there must be an absolute sale, properly documented, with no reservation of interest by you (other than the loan from you to the trust to finance the purchase). If you are going to reserve an interest in the property, this must normally be done before the sale of the asset to the trust. As taxation and estate duty laws vary from country to country, expert advice is always needed.

You can sell as much as you like to the trust at the one time — that is a sale and not a gift. In all cases, a sliding value clause must be included in both the sale and purchase agreements and the Deeds of Acknowledgment of Debt. This increases (or reduces) the sale price of assets to their true market value as of the date of the sale, in the event of there being a challenge to the value at which those assets were sold. In New Zealand, the Commissioner of Inland Revenue has accepted that where a sliding value clause is used 'gift duty will not be payable'.[2]

THE FORMALITIES NEEDED TO LEGALLY TRANSFER OWNERSHIP OF ASSETS FROM YOU TO THE TRUST VARY FROM COUNTRY TO COUNTRY

The documents needed to legally transfer ownership of assets from you to the trust will vary according to the asset, and the laws of the country in which the asset is situated. Specialist advice is therefore needed on the formalities required in each of the countries in which the trust has assets. For example, in order to legally transfer real estate owned under the Torrens system (that is, all New Zealand real estate and real estate in some Australian states), a Memorandum of Transfer must be registered at the Land Titles Office.[3] The sale is not complete until registration of the transfer.[4] Generally, interests in land which are not under the Torrens system can only be transferred by a deed of conveyance signed by the person transferring the property.

FAILURE TO LEGALLY TRANSFER OWNERSHIP OF ASSETS TO THE TRUSTEES OF THE TRUST

It is vitally important that the dotting of i's and crossing of t's necessary to transfer ownership to the trustees are completed. If the documentation needed to transfer your interest in the assets to the trustees is not completed, there is a resulting trust back in favour of the settlor, that is, the trustees hold the assets in trust for you.[5]

IOUs IN EXCHANGE FOR THE SALE OF THE ASSETS

As described on page 117, in exchange for the sale of your assets to the trust, the trust will give you an IOU (Deed of Acknowledgment of Debt). In other words, you have one hundred percent vendor-financed the trust's purchase of the assets.

The terms of the Deed of Acknowledgment of Debt will vary from country to country and will be determined by the taxation laws of the country in which you reside. In New Zealand, such loans will normally be upon demand, with interest payable at a rate to be agreed upon (or at bank rates if an agreement cannot be reached), but only if demanded in writing by a set date each year.

What is vitally important to realise is that the IOU you get back from the trust will decrease in value with inflation.

If I gave you a bank guarantee, would you lend me $500,000, interest free, for twenty years? The answer is clearly no, as when I give you back the $500,000 in twenty years' time, it will be worth a lot less. This is the reason why money you lend to the trust decreases in value over time.

WHY FUTURE INCREASES IN THE VALUE OF THE ASSETS BELONG TO THE TRUST

On the other hand, as the trust now owns the assets, all increases in the value of the assets now belong to the trust. It is like you borrowing from a lender. The lender does not receive any part of the increase in value of the asset it has security over.

SUMMARY

→ You have made the trust a loan to enable it to buy your assets.

→ By selling your assets to the trust and receiving an IOU, the trust gets the benefit of future increases in the value of the assets. On the other hand, you are getting progressively poorer as the value of your IOU goes down in value over time.[6]

14

SUCCESS WITH INVESTMENTS

The key to investing is not assessing how much an industry is going to affect society, or how much it will grow, but rather determining the competitive advantage of any given company and, above all, the durability of that advantage.

WARREN BUFFETT, AT HERB ALLEN'S
SUN VALLEY, IDAHO, RETREAT, JULY 1999

SUCCESS WITH INVESTMENTS

This book is a book about success. Success involves learning about success with investments.

Warren Buffett says, 'Success in investing doesn't correlate with IQ once you're above the IQ level of 25. Once you have ordinary intelligence, what you need is the temperament to control the urges that get other people into trouble in investing.'[1] Robert Kiyosaki and Sharon Lechter[2] point out that success with investments will not come about through working hard, having children, buying a bigger house, getting paid more and as a result being taxed more, saving for children's future education and saving for retirement.

The good news is that by tapping into the great pool of information available on wealth creation, and by adopting the bold new ideas of the rich, we can all succeed far better than we would have done otherwise.

As discussed in chapter 1, the growth in the number of millionaires in recent generations shows both how well planning works, and how by adopting brave new entrepreneurial ideas it is possible for you to achieve your goals more effectively than you are now. The bad news is that if you stick to the old ways you cannot be as successful with your investments.

SUCCESS THROUGH THE TRUST OWNING
APPRECIATING INVESTMENTS

It is essential that all investments that will go up in value are owned by the trust so that they are kept safe. There is little point in accumulating wealth in your own name when unforeseen events could take it from you. You cannot guarantee that you will achieve your important objectives. You have a choice between keeping your fingers crossed and hoping, or investing safely through a trust.

WHY KEEPING INCOME-PRODUCING INVESTMENTS IN YOUR OWN NAME REDUCES YOUR ASSET PROTECTION PLANNING OPPORTUNITIES

Remember, your objective is personal poverty and a rich trust. You are only getting wealthier as a result of making savings from investment income or business. As your personal investments go up in value so does your wealth (though it should be noted that bank deposits do not go up in value). You cannot achieve your objectives of personal poverty and a rich trust if you are making personal capital gains on assets you have not sold to the trust.

In both cases you will always be increasing your wealth. This occurs because the overall asset protection programme has not been carefully thought out (often because it has not been prepared by an expert).

SUMMARY

→ By tapping into the great pool of information available on wealth creation, and by adopting the bold new ideas of the rich, we can become far more successful at achieving our objectives.

→ What is essential is that all investments are owned by the trust so that they are kept safe.

→ You cannot achieve your objective of personal poverty and a rich trust if you are making personal capital gains on assets you have not sold to the trust or savings from the income generated by such investments. In both cases, you will always be increasing your wealth.[3]

15

SUCCESS IN BUSINESS

Set your expectations high; find men and women
whose integrity and values you respect;
get their agreement on a course of action;
and give them your ultimate trust.

JOHN AKERS

SUCCESS IN BUSINESS

What the self-starters mentioned in chapter 2 have shown is that we can all take control of our future by looking for bold new business ideas, positive action and positive planning — business planning, investment planning, and asset protection and trust planning. Certainly some of us will do it better than others, but we can all learn how to plan much better than we do now.

THE SKILLS YOU NEED TO SUCCEED IN BUSINESS

Going into business is an important decision. A large proportion of first businesses fail. According to the Australian Bureau of Statistics, as many as 90 percent of new businesses fail within five years. It is critical that before deciding to go into business you ensure that you have the personal qualities and support needed to own and operate a business. You will need to plan very carefully if you are to succeed, and prepare yourself — and your family — for the challenges of running your own business.

I have been running businesses since 1975. From my experience, I believe that a successful business owner must have:

- confidence in their ability to succeed,
- a need for feelings of accomplishment and achievement,
- a desire for responsibility,
- a desire to work hard,
- a high energy level,

- a high degree of commitment,
- total dedication to the business,
- strong organisational skills,
- the ability to be flexible,
- a desire for immediate feedback,
- a willingness to seek expert advice,
- a tolerance for uncertainty,
- a preference for moderate risk.

If you do not have these characteristics, as well as a great product or service and a strong market demand for your product or service, you should not go into business.

Before starting a business it is essential that you research your business proposal. Satisfy yourself that the business will be more profitable than your current job and prepare a written business and financial plan for your proposed business.

Having decided to go into business there are a number of steps you should take. These include selecting a business which you have the skills to run, and establishing the best way to begin.

HOW TO GET STARTED IN BUSINESS

If you have the above characteristics and a strong market demand for your product or services then you should do the following:

- Learn as much as you can about your proposed business. Ask questions. Join industry associations.
- Find a lawyer, accountant, banker, and insurance agent and consult them as required. Always take advice from experts.

✴ Study successful competitors carefully.

✴ Write a business plan to help you budget properly and minimise risk.

✴ Realise that starting a business will take more money than you think.

✴ Arrange necessary loans.

✴ Make sure that you can secure a good location, and that it can be modified to suit your needs (if necessary).

✴ Make sure that you can obtain necessary licences and permits in that location.

✴ Order stock and supplies to run the business.

✴ Make your customers happy and keep them coming back.

✴ Put a great marketing plan in place. So few businesses actually ask for orders. Look at how much employees at McDonalds sell by asking you whether you want to order more items. Do the same. Prepare a checklist of the products or services that your customers will need and run through it with them. For example, if you have a paintshop, the checklist would include paint, different types of brushes for the various parts of the painting job, filler, sandpaper, paint remover, drop sheets, and so on. The customers will thank you and buy more, simply because you asked them in a very helpful manner.

✴ Keep detailed records of customers. Follow up with business cards and promotional offers. It is easier to sell to satisfied customers than to people who do not know you. Very few businesses market to existing customers.

✴ Be willing to work long and hard. Forty-hour weeks are now a thing of the past.

✴ Run it yourself. No one will look after your business like you.

✴ Hire good, experienced employees.

✳ You will inevitably suffer disappointment and frustration. You must be determined to come back from disappointment more determined to succeed.

✳ Keep complete and accurate records for tax purposes, for your banking needs, and for your own guidance.

✳ Obtain insurances; arrange utilities and phone services.

✳ Set up a record keeping system.

✳ In New Zealand, contact your Chamber of Commerce for details of the small business seminars they run. In Australia, federal, state and local governments offer advice, courses and practical assistance to help you start your business.

WHY PERSONALLY OWNING SHARES IN YOUR PRIVATE COMPANY REDUCES YOUR ASSET PROTECTION PLAN OPPORTUNITIES

Make sure the business is set up so it is a continuation of your strategy of personal poverty and a rich trust. The odds are that if you are sued, both you personally and your company will be sued as first and second defendants. Under these circumstances, having a private company owned by you personally will give you little more protection than running the business in your own name.

In New Zealand, asset protection is obtained only three years after the making of each gift. However, you do get protection against all increases in the value of the trust's assets from day one (so long as you are solvent at that time). Accordingly, the sooner you put in place an asset protection programme the more likely it is that you will benefit from it. In addition, if you own all the shares in your private company and are paying all the income to yourself/selves as shareholder salaries, you maximise your personal wealth.

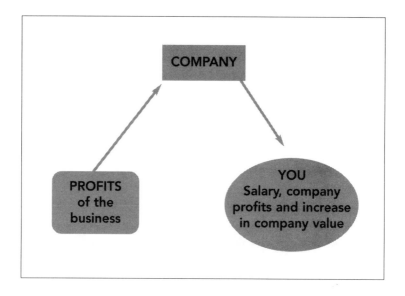

Remember Bill and Joy (see chapter 3)? They became personally wealthy because they sold only their family home to the trust when they set up their company (then worth $200,000). By 1995 the company was worth $500,000. In 1995 they sold the company to the trust for $500,000 and, in addition, also sold the investments represented by profits from the company of $500,000 to the trust, a total of $1 million. As they put it, 'What would have taken us four years to gift at a value of $200,000 will now take us twenty years to gift.'

You cannot achieve your objective of personal poverty and a rich trust if you are getting wealthier as a result of personal savings out of private company income or personally owned shares in your private company increasing in value. This puts everything at risk. By accumulating all wealth in your personal name, you are in fact doing your best to ensure that you will lose as much as possible (probably everything) in the event of a business collapse.

Don't forget that your business can fail because of factors beyond your control, including people failing to pay you, employee mistakes, penalties under Acts, and damages awards.

> Jim was a plumbing contractor. Like most of his mates he was not wealthy and was told by his lawyer that he did not need a trust. 'I only owned my home (worth $200,000) and my plumbing business (worth $50,000). In good years I was only earning $60,000. My lawyer told me that people with these assets did not need trusts. I believed him.' Jim thought he was made when he secured a $500,000 plumbing contract for some waterfront apartments. He hired more workers and bought more vehicles and equipment, borrowing against his home. 'The contractor paid me fine for the first month. Then delays in receiving payments started. The contractor made all sorts of excuses as to why payments were late. Then payments stopped.' The contractor was placed in liquidation as the company couldn't pay its bills. It owed other businesses $4 million and had assets of only $1 million. Only the secured creditors, such as the contractor's bank, got anything. 'I owed my subcontractors $200,000, and owed my bank $100,000. I had to sell my house to pay off the bank and 50 percent of my other bills. It is likely that I will now be bankrupted as I still owe $100,000 and have nothing to pay it with.'

If you set up a trust as part of an asset protection plan well before such disasters occur, the trust's investments will not all be lost. The sooner you start the more your assets will be protected.

SUCCESS THROUGH A TRUST OWNING
THE SHARES IN THE COMPANY

Never forget that your objective is personal poverty and a rich trust. To achieve this you sell most of the shares in your company to a trust for their current value (as determined by your accountant). In New Zealand, to avoid the need to deduct PAYE tax, it is normal for you to retain one share so that you can

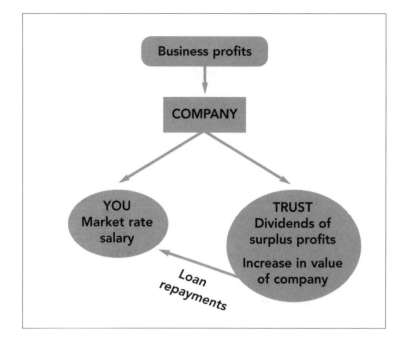

continue to be a shareholder employee, if you wish, paying provisional tax as you did before.

The minutes of both the trust and the company must record the shares that have been transferred. As legal requirements differ from country to country, expert advice must be taken to ensure that the correct legal formalities for the transfer of ownership of the shares to the trust have been completed.

Genuinely treat the company as if it is owned by someone else. For that reason, if you operate your business through a company (depending upon the taxation laws of your country), you should be paid only the market rate that you would pay someone else to carry out your job. If necessary, an employment consultant can advise you on what that market rate is.

In the event of your new income being insufficient for your purposes, you simply request loan repayments from the trust (which would be funded from the dividend payments being received by the trust). These loan repayments will accelerate the rate at which the loan owed to you by the trust is reduced, thereby accelerating your gifting programme, as the following shows.

	Without a trust	With a trust
Income after tax	$150,000	$50,000
Expenditure	-($80,000)	-($80,000)
Net income less expenditure	$70,000	-($30,000)
Loan owned by trust	$540,000	$540,000
Loan repayments from trust to fund living costs/savings from investment	$70,000	-($30,000)
Gift	-($27,000)	-($27,000)
Balance of loan	$583,000	$483,000

	Without a trust	With a trust	Additional asset protection achieved
Net assets at end of year 1	$583,000	$483,000	$100,000
Net assets at end of year 2	$626,000	$430,000	$196,000
Net assets at end of year 3	$673,000	$377,000	$296,000

The example shows that by living off capital (loan repayments from the trust), you can get poorer faster.

The trust should also own the shareholder's loans made by you to the company. Again, for credibility the trust should normally charge the company commercial interest rates on these loans. This means that the trust receives interest income without company taxation having been deducted from it. That income can then be distributed, as is appropriate, by the trustees to beneficiaries who are on lower taxation rates. Depending on taxation laws, consideration should be given to the trust leasing to the company all plant and equipment at normal lease rates (with the same income splitting consequences).

The other reason for ensuring that the company has minimal assets of its own is for asset protection purposes. For the same reason, the trust should consider taking debenture security over the company to ensure that it is a preferential creditor, ranking ahead of unsecured creditors. This is particularly important for high risk professionals such as doctors, dentists, engineers, architects and others who can be sued for substantial sums (including exemplary or punitive damages). Shareholders are entitled to the surplus profits of the company, and will normally be paid those profits by way of a dividend. The trust is now the shareholder, and is now entitled to those surplus profits. In New Zealand surplus profits have dividend imputation credits attached. In Australia, there are franking credits. When the shareholders receive their dividend they get the benefit of the tax already being paid and they can offset that against their own taxation liability.

In this manner the trust will make the savings which you would otherwise have made, and therefore have the ability to make the investments which you would otherwise have made, from the resulting savings. The company will then pay tax at company rates on what would otherwise have been the balance of your personal income. The trend in a number of countries, including Australia, is to lower the rate of company tax.

If your income is not reduced in this manner, then the savings made from your income could exceed your gifting ability with the result that you could be going backwards in terms of your asset protection plan, rather than forwards.

COMPANIES FOR PROFESSIONALS

Many professionals are now able to run their businesses under the umbrella of a private company.

In New Zealand, the medical and dental professions have changed their rules to allow doctors and dentists to practise as companies. Also in New Zealand, lawyers are among the few professionals who cannot run their businesses through a company (for reasons only their antiquated governing bodies understand).

In order to achieve the safety that personal poverty and a rich trust brings, professionals who have the opportunity of running their practice through a company have no option but to do so, and have no alternative other than to form a trust to own the shares in that private company. This is for the asset protection reasons mentioned above.

In New Zealand, some lawyers now accept cases on a contingency fee basis (just as occurs in America). Litigation lawyers nowadays have no hesitation in taking cases against professionals for substantial sums. The public are also becoming more litigious.

SUCCESS THROUGH HAVING A SUCCESSION PLAN FOR YOUR BUSINESS

You must also have a succession plan for your business. If you become incapacitated or die, will your business survive? Will your partner or children be able to continue running it? By planning for these possibilities you do your best to ensure the continued success of your business.

On the death of you and your partner (if you have one), is leaving the business to all of your children fair? Are they all capable of running the business or will it be complicated by disagreement? Fairness and equality are not the same. It may be better to leave the business to the child or children capable of running it, and leave assets of similar value to the others. In each of the above cases, advance planning avoids such problems.

SUMMARY

→ You cannot achieve your objective of personal poverty and a rich trust if you are getting wealthier as a result of personal savings out of private company income, or if the personally owned shares in your private company are increasing in value. This puts everything at risk. When a trust owns most of the shares in the company and the shareholder's loan accounts, you gain the safety of protecting non-business assets, and will achieve your goal of personal poverty and a rich trust.

16

SUCCESS WITH PROPERTY AND REALTY

*I do not believe in a fate that falls on men
however they act; but I do believe in a fate
that falls on them unless they act.*

G.K. CHESTERTON

SUCCESS WITH PROPERTY AND
REALTY INVESTMENTS

We can all take control of our futures by looking for bold new business ideas, positive action and positive planning — this includes planning your property and realty investments. The three most important factors in determining whether or not you are making a good property investment are location, location and location. A given property may be worth thousands more than an equivalent property in the same city, just because of its address. In the case of your home, if you think that you won't be living in a particular location very long, you might choose to live in a smaller house in an appreciating neighbourhood, rather than in a larger house in a declining neighbourhood, because of resale value.

Planning is essential. Always begin your search for a property with the end in mind. Picture what you are trying to achieve. What will life be like when you get there? How will it be better than what you own now? Having a goal in front of you at all times energises you to achieve it, in spite of setbacks and frustrations.

Don't be influenced by cosmetic appeal. Look for sound construction first. Quality buildings have a 'feel' about them. With a little practice, you can learn to sense it. To get the best property you can for the least amount of money, make sure you are in the strongest possible negotiating position. Price is only one bargaining chip and it is not necessarily the most important one. Often other matters, such as the financial position of the buyer or the length of the conditional period, are critical to a seller. If you need to borrow, the way to make a strong offer is to be pre-approved by a lender. This involves the lender approving a loan subject only to a valuation of the property you want to buy.

If you have a property to sell, sell it before selecting a property to buy. If you make an offer subject to the sale of your own property you cannot negotiate the vendor down as much as you could with a cash offer. If you then have to sell your property quickly, you may not sell it for as much. The bottom line is that buying before selling might cost you tens of thousands of dollars.

SUCCESS THROUGH THE TRUST OWNING PROPERTY AND REALTY

Personal poverty and a rich trust are your objectives and for these reasons all properties, including your home, should be sold to the trust, unless there are cost or taxation reasons which prevent this.

In New Zealand there is no capital gains tax and your home should normally be owned by the trust. Presently, in Australia, the home in which you live is exempt from capital gains tax if it is owned by you, but in some cases not if it is owned by a discretionary trust. This is of course only relevant if you are going to (or might) sell the home. If it is to be kept in the family for generations, this may not be an issue. If, for taxation reasons, the trust cannot own the home it should lend you the money to buy it. In that way, your only asset will be the increase in value of the home.

IS RENTING A HOME A BETTER OPTION FOR YOU?

For some, renting a home will be the best option. You may not be economically or emotionally ready to own a home, or may have better investment options.

Advantages of renting include:

✴ maintenance and repairs are handled by the owner,

✴ it is easy to move,

✴ you have few responsibilities,

✴ your funds are not tied up in the house, and are available for other investments which may be more profitable than owning a home,

✴ your rent is normally fixed, making it easier to budget,

✴ you will make no loss on investment, as you do not own the home.

Some disadvantages are:

✴ there are no potential gains if the property goes up in value,

✴ improvements cannot be made or are limited,

✴ rent normally rises with inflation, except where there are many rental properties available,

✴ there will usually be restrictions on noise level or pet ownership.

BUYING A HOME

Buying a home offers the following advantages:

✴ the trust is forced to make savings by being forced to make mortgage repayments,

✴ the equity in the home improves the trust's credit status and its ability to borrow for other investments,

✴ if the property increases in value over a period of years the trust's assets increase in value,

✴ ownership may contribute to security, especially in retirement years when income normally decreases,

✴ more space may be available for family members and their activities,

✴ you have the freedom to make improvements and changes to the house and grounds as you wish.

The disadvantages of buying a home include:

✴ a substantial deposit may be needed,

✴ you will have to make a big commitment in time, emotion, and money,

✴ you may have limited money for other purchases or activities as your money is tied up in the home,

✴ you have to pay for maintenance and repairs which may be costly and take a great deal of time and effort,

✴ you have to pay for insurance, local authority rates and taxes (if any), the costs of which tend to increase with inflation,

✴ the home may become too large after children leave and may have to be sold,

✴ if you lose your income due to job termination or unemployment, you may not be able to afford the home ownership costs (unless you insure against this risk).

HOW MUCH HOUSE CAN YOU AFFORD?

Three considerations to take into account in determining how much house you can afford are the amount of take-home pay your family has, your family's living costs and other debt payments, and the total cost of housing expenses, including taxes, insurance, energy, furnishings, maintenance, and mortgage payments. You should find out about your lender's guidelines and then apply them to your circumstances.

WHEN IS THE BEST TIME
TO BUY A HOUSE?

The answer is not simple. Considerations need to be made as to what the local housing market is like now and what is it likely to be like in several years. Is it a buyer's or a seller's market? What is happening and is likely to happen to the local economy? Are houses in the neighbourhood increasing in value? Will you be able to sell the house for a profit if you decide to move?

BEFORE BUYING IDENTIFY THE FACTORS ABOUT
A HOME THAT ARE IMPORTANT TO YOU

Buying a house can be a great experience if you plan, but it can be a financial disaster if you do not. Your final decision is a complicated one, often based on emotional as well as financial factors. Look only at houses in the price range you can afford. If you look at houses which are more expensive than you can afford, you will never be happy with those that you can afford.

Decide on the space you need and the location, community services, and any other personal needs you have. Think about what you really need instead of what you would like. If you are a couple or have children, ask every family member who is old enough to make their own list. Compare the lists then combine them (using compromise) to make a single list for the family. Your list should include answers to the following questions:

⚹ What are you going to use the home for?

⚹ Is it the right size and does it have the features needed to meet your requirements?

⚹ Are you likely to need more or less space in the next five years? Ten years?

⚹ Does the home give the amount of privacy you require? Can it be altered to provide enough privacy? Do you want more open space, as in the country?

⚹ What sort of neighbourhood is it in? Is the area in which the home is located is going up or down in value.

⚹ Are the area and the home safe and secure?

⚹ Do the residents of surrounding properties have similar occupational and social interests?

⚹ What is the condition of the property. When house-hunting, keep in mind the difference between 'skin' and 'bones'. The bones are things that cannot be changed, such as the location, view, size of the section, noise in the area, school district and floor plan. The skin represents easily changed surface finishes like carpet, wallpaper, colour, and window coverings. Buy the house with good bones, because the skin can always be changed to match your tastes. Imagine each house as if it were vacant. Consider each house's underlying merits, not the seller's decorating skills.

⚹ How much time do you have to spend on maintenance and upkeep? Do you have the time and/or skills to meet the home's maintenance requirements? When looking at an existing house learn as much as you can about the condition of the house to see if repairs will need to be made.

⚹ How well is the area serviced by police, hospitals and fire stations?

⚹ Is the property connected to sanitation services, water supplies and so on?

- What community services are available, for example, garbage pick-up, milk and mail delivery?
- How far are you willing to travel to work, school, church, or shopping?
- Is there easy access to public transport?

With regard to the suitability of the property for your requirements, consider the following:

- Do the bedrooms and bathrooms have enough space and privacy?
- Is the kitchen and work area well planned?
- Are there adequate work and storage areas?
- Are the dining and living areas adequate for family entertaining and resting?
- Is storage adequate and well placed in each area of the house?
- Do the room sizes, shapes and wall areas permit use of your existing or planned furnishings and equipment?
- Are the interior and exterior finishes acceptable, and in a condition that is good and easy to maintain?
- Is there adequate and efficient heating and lighting?
- Is outdoor space sufficient for your needs, for example, patio, deck, lawn and garden space, and outdoor storage?

The layout of the house, traffic flow, and the division of the space affects how your family lives in a house and how the members relate to one another. Roughly sketch the floor plan of the house you are looking at. Try to identify the traffic patterns in the house. Try to place your furniture and possessions on the floor plan, and picture how your family will live in the house. One way to do this is to mentally go through your family's morning routine. Visualise where traffic jams or problems might occur. Pick out other events that regularly occur in your family and visualise those events in that space. Will the rooms fit your family's needs? Will the space adapt to your needs as family needs change?

Is storage located where your family will need it, and is it adequate for the kinds of items that your family has to store? Is there space for cleaning equipment, hobby and sports equipment, and seasonal items? Compare the storage space in the house you are looking at with the space in the place you now live in. Is there adequate bathroom space to accommodate your family during rush-hour traffic? Research has shown that this is a critical factor in levels of family stress.

The kitchen is often the most-used space in a house. Look for adequate work spaces, storage near major appliances, and a good arrangement for the appliances.

Four out of five people will eventually have some physical problem that could make it difficult to live independently. In addition, your elderly parents or other relatives may need to live with you in the future. Few existing houses are designed to accommodate people with disabilities such as mobility, vision or hearing impairment. A house that meets standards for accessibility can benefit many people. Consider ways to adapt the house, should the need arise.

To buy or to build?

Factors that will affect your decision to buy or to build include the supply of houses available that suit your family, the location you wish to live in, and the time within which you must move. Some people find that the many decisions that must be made when building a house are so time-consuming that they would rather not spend the time and energy it takes to build. Normally, an existing house is less expensive than buying or building a new one.

BUYING A PREVIOUSLY OWNED HOUSE

There are usually more older houses than newly built ones on the market. One of the benefits of buying an existing house is that you can see and meet the people who live there, and see the quality of the neighbourhood. You can also see if the community services which you need, such as shopping, schools and churches, are available and convenient. Another advantage is that many fixtures and furnishings are often already in place and are sold with the house. Landscaping has usually been completed, which may save you time, effort and money. When considering existing houses, you (or an expert employed by you) must check for the following:

✴ Structural defects. Check foundations for cracks or watermarks. Examine the condition of the floor joists (wall-to-wall supports) and structural beams. Are there cracks in the foundations?

✴ Examine the house from the outside. Does the roof sag? If so, examine the rafters in the attic. Is the roof ridge (the line at the top of the roof) straight?

✴ Inside the house, check the floors to see if they are level. You can check whether a floor is level with a marble. It should not roll when placed on a vinyl or wood floor. Uneven floors could be a sign of settling due to age, or it could mean problems with supporting joists. What is the condition of the window frames?

✴ Signs of water damage. Look for discoloured ceilings or walls, mildew odours, stains or discolouration, or evidence of replastering or retiling in just one area of a room. Check under the house for damp ground or standing water.

✴ If the house has a basement, look for water stains or dampness on the walls and floors. Check the gutters and downspouts for clear drainage. Is there a musty smell (a sign of moisture)?

- Does the section slope away from the house (enough to carry water away from it)?
- Lack of water pressure. You can test this by flushing toilets and turning on hot and cold water taps at the same time.
- Do the doors shut tightly?
- Is the floor solid or does it squeak?
- Faulty plumbing. Ask what kind of pipes are installed and how old they are. Some older houses have pipes that may have corroded over time and become clogged. Have the system checked for the presence of lead in the water, which can be a health risk.
- If there is a septic system, ask when it was last inspected and cleaned. Stand near the tank and see if any odour comes from it or if there are any soggy areas around it.
- Inadequate wiring. If you are unfamiliar with wiring, a professional inspector can answer your questions. Look for obvious signs of electrical malfunctions, such as lights that flicker or don't work. Note the number and placement of electrical outlets. Most experts recommend at least two outlets for each room.
- Energy efficiency. In a home that is not energy efficient, your air conditioning and heating bills could be higher than your mortgage repayment. Take time to check last year's air conditioning and heating bills. Find out whether any supplemental heat sources, like space heaters, were used.
- Air conditioning and furnace. Ask the seller's fuel dealer or furnace service company to verify the condition of the furnace and whether it is adequate for the size of the house.
- Insulation. New houses generally have insulation in the walls, under the floor and in the ceiling. However, many older houses do not. Ask if any insulation has been added and where.
- Environmental inspections. Poor indoor air quality may cause or contribute to health problems, especially for the very young,

the elderly, and the disabled. To be sure that you are buying a safe and healthy house, you need to know which products and pollutants you cannot tolerate. High or continuous levels of indoor pollutants may result from the location; the materials, products and environmental conditions within the house itself; or the practices and activities of the people who live there.

✹ Asbestos may be found in older homes in walls and ceiling insulation, in textured paints, acoustic ceiling tiles, home appliances, and wrapped around hot water and steam pipes and heating ducts. Removal should always be performed by a professional.

✹ Radon is a colourless, odourless, radioactive gas that comes from the ground. Continual exposure to elevated levels of radon increases the risk of lung cancer. A simple radon test will indicate the presence of the gas.

✹ Lead contamination in a house is usually the result of lead-based paint or plumbing systems with brass fixtures that contain lead, lead pipe, or lead-based solder in pipe joints. Lead-based paint chips can be particularly dangerous to small children.

✹ Buried fuel storage tanks, waste dumpsites, salvage yards, industrial sites or agricultural operations can create hazards that may remain hidden for many years. An environmental inspection of the site and survey of the history of the area may help identify potential hazards.

Don't confuse maintenance problems with poor construction. A house can be in need of a facelift and be basically sound. A careful assessment of the physical and environmental conditions of a house before purchase can save you time, money, and heartache. If you are in doubt about the construction or safety of a house or section that you particularly like, hire a professional housing inspector. The price you pay for this service could save you thousands of dollars. Some problems can only be detected by professionals like housing inspectors.

Buying an existing house to renovate can have a number of pitfalls. The biggest one is overspending for the neighbourhood or location. The value of adding on and major renovation can be uncertain. Always obtain expert advice as to whether the proposed renovations will increase the value of the home.

NEW HOUSES

New houses may be better insulated, have more energy efficient appliances and heating and cooling systems, have up-to-date electrical wiring and plumbing systems, and will generally be more maintenance free than older houses. They usually have more modern facilities, such as larger bathrooms and closets and state of the art kitchens. Depending on the location, local authority rates and taxes (if any) in newly developed subdivisions may be less than in some existing neighbourhoods. Try to determine whether homes in the area where you want to build are appreciating in value as this will affect resale value. Building inspectors do not always catch problems with construction. When you are building, you need to pay close attention to the construction process.

SUMMARY

→ Personal poverty and a rich trust are your objectives. For that reason your house should be sold to the trust, unless there are cost or taxation reasons that make this unwise.

→ You do not need an occupation lease unless you are rich and need to reduce the value of your home for estate duty reasons.[1]

A P P E N D I X

Table A

Present value of annuity or other interest for life of male or expectant on death of male

Years of age	Expectation of life of male (years)	Present value of $1 per annum for life	Present value of $1 payable on death	Present value of income on capital of $1 for life
30	41.89	17.40904	0.12955	0.87045
31	40.96	17.28896	0.13555	0.86445
32	40.03	17.16314	0.14184	0.85816
33	39.10	17.03125	0.14844	0.85156
34	38.17	16.89325	0.15534	0.84466
35	37.24	16.74887	0.16256	0.83744
36	36.32	16.59947	0.17003	0.82997
37	35.40	16.44326	0.17784	0.82216
38	34.48	16.27992	0.18600	0.81400
39	33.57	16.11105	0.19445	0.80555
40	32.65	15.93259	0.20337	0.79663
41	31.74	15.74811	0.21259	0.78741
42	30.83	15.55535	0.22223	0.77777
43	29.92	15.35394	0.23230	0.76770
44	29.02	15.14570	0.24271	0.75729
45	28.13	14.92971	0.25351	0.74649
46	27.25	14.70681	0.26466	0.73534
47	26.38	14.47697	0.27615	0.72385
48	25.52	14.24019	0.28799	0.71201
49	24.67	13.99650	0.30018	0.69982
50	23.83	13.74593	0.31270	0.68730

continued

Years of age	Expectation of life of male (years)	Present value of $1 per annum for life	Present value of $1 payable on death	Present value of income on capital of $1 for life
51	23.00	13.48857	0.32557	0.67443
52	22.18	13.22161	0.33892	0.66108
53	21.38	12.95106	0.35245	0.64755
54	20.59	12.67399	0.36630	0.63370
55	19.82	12.39437	0.38028	0.61972
56	19.06	12.10793	0.39460	0.60540
57	18.32	11.81622	0.40919	0.59081
58	17.60	11.52338	0.42383	0.57617
59	16.89	11.22607	0.43870	0.56130
60	16.19	10.92067	0.45397	0.54603
61	15.50	10.60871	0.46956	0.53044
62	14.82	10.29307	0.48535	0.51465
63	14.16	9.97560	0.50122	0.49878
64	13.52	9.65621	0.51719	0.48281
65	12.90	9.34054	0.53297	0.46703
66	12.29	9.01705	0.54915	0.45085
67	11.71	8.70177	0.56491	0.43509
68	11.14	8.38437	0.58078	0.41922
69	10.59	8.06670	0.59666	0.40334
70	10.05	7.75097	0.61245	0.38755
71	9.53	7.43320	0.62834	0.37166
72	9.01	7.11396	0.64430	0.35570
73	8.51	6.79196	0.66040	0.33960
74	8.03	6.48255	0.67587	0.32413
75	7.57	6.17217	0.69139	0.30861
76	7.13	5.87436	0.70628	0.29372
77	6.71	5.58028	0.72099	0.27901
78	6.31	5.29600	0.73520	0.26480
79	5.92	5.01599	0.74920	0.25080

Table B

Present value of annuity or other interest for life of female or expectant on death of female

Years of age	Expectation of life of female (years)	Present value of $1 per annum for life	Present value of $1 payable on death	Present value of income on capital of $1 for life
30	45.06	17.78043	0.11098	0.88902
31	44.11	17.67502	0.11625	0.88375
32	43.16	17.56461	0.12177	0.87823
33	42.21	17.44898	0.12755	0.87245
34	41.26	17.32787	0.13361	0.86639
35	40.32	17.20238	0.13988	0.86012
36	39.38	17.07102	0.14645	0.85355
37	38.44	16.93352	0.15332	0.84668
38	37.50	16.78959	0.16052	0.83948
39	36.57	16.64058	0.16797	0.83203
40	35.64	16.48470	0.17576	0.82424
41	34.71	16.32162	0.18392	0.81608
42	33.79	16.15293	0.19235	0.80765
43	32.88	15.97856	0.20107	0.79893
44	31.97	15.79638	0.21018	0.78982
45	31.06	15.60540	0.21973	0.78027
46	30.17	15.40991	0.22950	0.77050
47	29.29	15.20817	0.23959	0.76041
48	28.41	14.99774	0.25011	0.74989
49	27.54	14.78078	0.26096	0.73904
50	26.68	14.55732	0.27213	0.72787
51	25.82	14.32456	0.28377	0.71623
52	24.98	14.08804	0.29560	0.70440
53	24.14	13.83998	0.30800	0.69200
54	23.31	13.58470	0.32077	0.67923

continued

Years of age	Expectation of life of female (years)	Present value of $1 per annum for life	Present value of $1 payable on death	Present value of income on capital of $1 for life
55	22.49	13.32253	0.33387	0.66613
56	21.67	13.05019	0.34749	0.65251
57	20.87	12.77449	0.36128	0.63872
58	20.08	12.49093	0.37545	0.62455
59	19.30	12.19839	0.39008	0.60992
60	18.53	11.89933	0.40503	0.59497
61	17.77	11.59402	0.42030	0.57970
62	17.02	11.28238	0.43588	0.56412
63	16.28	10.95993	0.45200	0.54800
64	15.56	10.63620	0.46819	0.53181
65	14.84	10.30270	0.48487	0.51513
66	14.14	9.96598	0.50170	0.49830
67	13.45	9.62085	0.51896	0.48104
68	12.77	9.27160	0.53642	0.46358
69	12.11	8.892159	0.55392	0.44608
70	11.46	8.56256	0.57187	0.42813
71	10.83	8.20702	0.58965	0.41035
72	10.22	7.85036	0.60748	0.39252
73	9.63	7.49459	0.62527	0.37473
74	9.07	7.15080	0.64246	0.35754
75	8.53	6.80486	0.65976	0.34024
76	8.01	6.46966	0.67652	0.32348
77	7.52	6.13833	0.69308	0.30692
78	7.05	5.82022	0.70899	0.29101
79	6.59	5.49499	0.72525	0.27475
80	6.16	5.18940	0.74053	0.25947

E N D NOTES

1 The rich achieve their objectives by planning

1 Gifting in Australia has no gift duty, therefore entire debts can be gifted at one time.

2 For those with Internet access, the Forbes 400 website can be found at: www.forbes.com

3 Fridson, Martin S., *How to be a Billionaire: Proven Strategies from the Titans of Wealth*, John Wiley & Sons.

4 See www.berkshirehathaway.com To find out how Warren Buffett succeeded, I recommend you read *Buffettology: The Previously Unexplained Techniques That Have Made Warren Buffett the World's Most Famous Investor*, by Mary Buffett and David Clark, published by Simon and Schuster. Also, see www.buffetwatch.com

5 See www.paulallen.com

6 See www.virgin.com

7 Other success stories can be found at: www.estate planning-trusts.com/business_successful.html

2 Success through identifying risks

1 *New Zealand Herald*, 23 January 1997, page A11.

2 *New Zealand Herald*, 27 February 1997, page A1.

3 The Success with Law section of www.estateplanning-trusts.com/legal_main.html is constantly being expanded to contain information about major legal topics, including property claims. It contains information from leading experts in each legal area.

4 See Success with Trusts at www.estateplanning-trusts.com/eptt_main.html. This section contains information on the taxation laws in different countries, and incorporates information from taxation experts. To visit a country's taxation department website, navigate to the section dealing with that

country and visit the taxation section, which is on the right hand side of the index at the top of your country page. The 'News' section contains information changes to taxation laws in a number of countries. In New Zealand, it also provides links to the Inland Revenue Department's website.

5 For criteria for differing countries, see the Government Departments and Ministries section of www.estateplanning-trusts.com/eptt_main.html

6 Social Security Act (1964), Section 69F(6).

7 In New Zealand, estate duty or inheritance tax is likely to be reintroduced (on assets of more than $400,000 using Labour's previous proposals and on assets of more than $500,000 using the Alliance's current proposals). If estate duty is brought back, it could cost you 40 percent of your assets (the old estate duty rate) if they are worth over $400,000. In New Zealand, Labour's policy is that no new taxes (including estate duty) will be introduced until after 2002.

8 Both the United Kingdom and the United States of America have estate duty.

5 Success through a will leaving assets to a trust

1 You can obtain updates to this section from the Success with Trusts section of www.estateplanning-trusts.com/eptt_main. html.

6 Success through recording and updating your objectives

1 See chapter 10 for technical information about trustees of the trust during your lifetime.

2 See *Sham Trusts* by Ross Holmes for the reasons a transaction may be described as a 'sham'.

3 One of the places you can obtain details of law changes and their effects on asset protection plans is the news page of www.estateplanning-trusts.com/news_main.html

7 Success through planning now

1 Details of anti-avoidance measures in your country may be obtained from the websites of your Social Welfare authority via www.estateplanning-trusts.com/eptt_main.html

2 A number of politicians have trusts, including New Zealand Prime Minister Helen Clark who disclosed in May 2000 that she is a beneficiary of a trust. The websites of political parties can be accessed from your country page in the Success with Trusts section of www.estateplanning-trusts.com/eptt_main. html.

3 You may wish to obtain updates to this chapter from the Success with Trusts section of www.estateplanning-trusts. com/ eptt_ main.html.

8 The steps to success through a comprehensive asset protection plan

1 You may wish to obtain updates to this chapter from the Success with Trusts section of www.estateplanning-trusts.com/ eptt_ main.html

9 Success through using an expert to prepare your asset protection plan

1 The old New Zealand Work and Income Support Service, later WINZ.

2 See *Hamilton* [1895] 2 Ch 370.

3 New Zealand Law Society Trusts Conference paper, page 165.

4 New Zealand Law Society Seminar Paper, pages 12 and 15.

5 Taken from the guidance notes supplied by a New Zealand law firm to its clients.

6 In addition, my firm sends a newsletter to asset protection clients to keep them up to date with significant changes in trust law, taxation law and Inland Revenue Department policy. If your advisor does not already do so, I suggest you make arrangements that he/she contact you when changes may be required.

7 Information on the latest developments affecting asset protection planning can be found on the 'News' page in the Success with Trusts planning section of www.estateplanning-trusts.com/news_main.html This page also offers an update notification service. Enter your email address where indicated and you will be notified of any updates.

10 What is a trust?

1 Underhill and Hayton, *Law of Trusts and Trustees* (14th ed.), page 1. The definition was approved by L.J. Romer in *Green v Russell* [1959] 2 Q.B. 226, page 241.

2 Keeton and Sheridan, *The Law of Trusts* (12th ed.), Bany Rose Law Publishers Limited, 1993, page 1.

3 Deacons, Graham and James, *The A-Z of Trusts*, (1999), Centre for Professional Development, paragraphs 1–1320, *F.C. of T. v Hobbs* [1952] 98 CLR 151 and *Truesdale v F.C. of T.* [1971] 120 CLR 353.

4 How trustees should make valid decisions: these matters are dealt with in greater detail in Holmes, Ross, *Asset Protection Planning, Trusts and the Administration of Trusts.*

5 This was decided by the Privy Council in *C.S.D. v Perpetual Trustee Co. Ltd* [1943] A.C. 425, [1943] 1 All ER 525. The decision was followed by the *House of Lords in St Aubyn (LM) and Others v Attorney General* (No. 2) [1951] 2 All ER 473) and in *Oakes v C.S.D.* [1954] A.C. 57, [1953] 2 All ER 1563.

6 *Oakes v C.S.D.* [1954] A.C. 57, [1953] 2 All ER 1563. In Oakes, the settlor was the sole trustee and one of five beneficiaries.

7 Conveyancing Act 1919 (NSW), section 151A; Minors (Property and Contracts) Act 1970 (NSW), section 10(1)(b).

8 Lord Normand in the *Dundee Hospitals case* [1952] 1 All ER 896 at 900.

9 *Scott and Others v National Trust for Places of Historic Interest or Natural Beauty and Another* [1998] 2 All ER 705; Dundee General Hospitals Board of Management v Walker and Another [1952] 1 All ER 896 per Lord Reid at 904.

10 The practical requirements of this rule were summed up by Robert Walker in *Scott and Others v National Trust for Places of Historic Interest or Natural Beauty and Another* [1998] 2 All ER 705 at 717 to 719.

11 *Target Holdings Ltd v Redferns* (a firm) [1995] 3 All ER 785, [1996] AC 421 at 434.

12 *Clough v Bond* [1838] 3 Myl Cr 490.

13 *Edge and Others v Pensions Ombudsman and Another* [1998] 2 All ER 547 at page 567 Sir Richard Scott V-C.

14 *Gartside v I.R.C.* [1968] A.C. 553, [1968] 1 All ER 121.

15 *Kerns v Hill* [1990] 21 NSWLR 107 and re: Irving [1975]. 66 DLR 387.

16 *Manisty's Settlement* [1973] 2 All ER 1203 and re: Hay's *Settlement Trust* [1981] 3 All ER 786.

17 *Sham Trusts* by Ross Holmes deals with this topic in detail.

18 1st ed., 1954 p vii, preface.

19 The matters in this chapter are a summary of the detailed information contained in *Asset Protection Planning, Trusts and the Administration of Trusts* by Ross Holmes. For advisors, detailed technical information can be obtained from Butterworth's *Law of Trusts*.

11 Success through making sure that your asset protection plan works

1 After you have read this book you may wish to obtain updates to this chapter from the Success with Trusts section of www.estate planning-trusts.com

12 Success through getting poor ASAP

1 Refer to the policy statement in Tax Information Bulletin Vol. 6, No. 7 (December 1994), pages 10–12 for more detailed guidelines on the application of section 72.

2 *CIR v Morris* [1958] NZLR 1126 and *McCathie v McCathie* [1971] NZLR 58, decisions of the New Zealand Court of Appeal.

3 Section 4 of the Property Law Act 1952 (New Zealand).
4 *New Zealand Inland Revenue Department's Gift Duty. A guide for practitioners.* (IR 195 May 1999) Page 15 and *Case T20* [1997] 18 NZTC 8, 116.
5 P.O. Box 2871, Christchurch, telephone (03) 363 1858.
6 As detailed in their binding ruling in the *Tax Information Bulletin*, Volume 7, No.8, February 1996, page 7.
7 This chart is kindly supplied by Kendons, Chartered Accountants of Lower Hutt.
8 See *Tax Information Bulletin*, Volume 7, No. 8, February 1996, page 9.
9 As detailed in *Tax Information Bulletin*, Volume 7, No. 8, February 1996, pages 7 and 8.
10 Under section CE1 (1)(e) of the Income Tax Act 1994.
11 See *Tax Information Bulletin*, Volume 7, No. 8, February 1996, pages 10 to 13 (this applies to dispositions of real property made between 1 April 1996 and 31 March 1999).
12 Section 2, the definitions of disposition of property and gift (which include the surrender of any estate or interest in property) and section 63.

13 Success through the trust buying your assets at today's values

1 See Lord Shaw in *Lord Strathcona Steamship Co. Limited v Dominion Coal Co. Limited* [1926] AC 108 at 124, [1925] All ER 87 at 95.
2 *Tax Information Bulletin*, Volume 7, No. 8, February 1996, page 9.
3 Section 41(2) of the Land Transfer Act 1952 (New Zealand) and section 41 Real Property Act (Australia).
4 *Montgomery and Rennie v Continental Bags (NZ) Limited and Another* [1972] NZLR 884, *Cope v Keene* [1968] 118 CLR 1, *The Privy Council in Knight Sugar Co Ltd v Alberta Railway & Irrigation Co* [1938] 1 All ER 266.

5 *Vandervell's Trusts, White v Vandervell Trustees and Inland Revenue Comrs* [1971] AC 912 (House of Lords).

6 You may wish to obtain updates to this chapter from the Success with Trusts section of www.estateplanning-trusts.com

14 Success with investments

1 *Business Week* interview, June 25 1999. To find out how multi-billionaire Warren Buffett succeeded, I recommend you read Mary Buffett and David Clark's book, *Buffettology*, and visit www.buffetwatch.com

2 In their excellent book *Rich Dad, Poor Dad*. *Rich Dad's Guide to Investing* (the sequel to *Rich Dad, Poor Dad*) is also worth reading to find out 'what the rich invest in that the poor and middle class do not'. What is particularly good about these books is that they are motivational — they may prod you from procrastination into action.

3 The Success with Investments section at www.estateplanning-trusts.com contains updates to this chapter and more information about how to plan to succeed with investments.

15 Success in business

1 Check the news page at www.estateplanning-trusts.com and take expert advice as tax laws have a horrible habit of being changed.

16 Success with property and realty

1 The Success with Property and Realty section of www.estate planning-trusts.com contains advice on how to plan to succeed before purchasing property.

BIBLIOGRAPHY

Books, magazines and papers

Buffett, Mary and Clark, David, *Buffettology: The Previously Unexplained Techniques That Have Made Warren Buffett the World's Most Famous Investor*. Simon and Schuster, Pocket Books, London, 1999.

Business Week, June 25 1999.

Butterworths Law of Trusts. Butterworths, Wellington, 2000.

Deacons, Graham and James, *The A-Z of Trusts*. Centre for Professional Development, Australia, 1999 (loose leaf).

Fridson, Martin S., *How to be a Billionaire: Proven Strategies from the Titans of Wealth*, John Wiley & Sons, USA, January 2000.

Holmes, Ross, *Sham Trusts*, Pacific Trusts, Auckland, 1999.

— *Asset Protection Planning, Trusts and the Administration of Trusts*. Reed Publishing (NZ) Ltd, Auckland, in press, 2001.

Keeton and Sheridan, *The Law of Trusts* (12th ed.). Bany Rose Law Publishers Limited, Australia, 1993.

Kiyosaki, Robert and Lechter, Sharon, *Rich Dad, Poor Dad*. TechPress Inc., Arizona, USA, 1997.

Kiyosaki, Robert and Lechter, Sharon, *Rich Dad's Guide to Investing*. TechPress Inc., Arizona, 2000.

New Zealand Herald, 23 January 1997.

New Zealand Herald, 27 February 1997.

New Zealand Law Society, Topical Trust Issues. Seminar paper, 1998.

New Zealand Law Society Trusts Conference, Administration of Trusts. Seminar paper, 1999.

Underhill and Hayton, *Law of Trusts and Trustees* (14th ed.), UK.

Potter, Donald Charles, *Potter and Monroe's Tax Planning with Precedents* (1st ed.), (out of print).

Legal documents and actions

Copies of Law Reports can be located in most University Law Libraries and Court libraries. Some of the more recent Australian Law Reports can be located on the Internet at www.rossholmes. co.nz/eptt_Australia.html#Courts.

Some of the more recent United Kingdom Law Reports can be located on the Internet at www.rossholmes.co.nz/eptt_uk.html #Courts

The key to location of the law reports in which the following cases can be found is as follows. The number after the date, for example, 2 Ch, refers to the volume number of that year's Law Report in which the case can be found.

AC	Appeal Cases, United Kingdom
All ER	All England Law Reports, United Kingdom
Ch and Ch D	Chancery Division, United Kingdom
CLR	Commonwealth Law Reports, Australia
DLR	Dominion Law Reports, Canada
NSWLR	New South Wales Law Reports, Australia
NZLR	New Zealand Law Reports, New Zealand
NZTC	New Zealand Taxation Cases, New Zealand

Case T20 [1997] 18 NZTC 8,116.

CIR v Morris [1958] NZLR 1126.

Clough v Bond [1838] 3 Myl Cr 490.

Cope v Keene [1968] 118 CLR 1.

CSD v Perpetual Trustee Co. Ltd [1943] AC 425, [1943] 1 All ER 525.

Dundee General Hospitals Board of Management v Walker and Another [1952] 1 All ER 896 per Lord Reid at 904.

Dundee Hospitals case [1952] 1 All ER 896 at 900.

Edge and Others v Pensions Ombudsman and Another [1998] 2 All ER 547.

Gartside v IRC [1968] AC 553, [1968] 1 All ER 121.

Hamilton [1895] 2 Ch 370.

House of Lords in St Aubyn (LM) and Others v Attorney General (No 2) [1951] 2 All ER 473.

Kerns v Hill [1990] 21 NSWLR 107.

Knight Sugar Co Ltd v Alberta Railway & Irrigation Co [1938] 1 All ER 266 (Privy Council).

Lord Strathcona Steamship Co. Limited v Dominion Coal Co. Limited [1926] AC 108 at 124, [1925] All ER 87 at 95.

Manisty's Settlement [1973] 2 All ER 1203.

McCathie v McCathie [1971] NZLR 58.

Montgomery and Rennie v Continental Bags (NZ) Limited and Another [1972] NZLR 884

New Zealand Inland Revenue Department, *Gift Duty. A guide for practitioners.* IR 195, May 1999, New Zealand.

Oakes v CSD [1954] AC 57, [1953] 2 All ER 1563.

Re: *Hay's Settlement Trust* [1981] 3 All ER 786.

Re: *Irving* [1975] 66 DLR 387.

Scott and Others v National Trust for Places of Historic Interest or Natural Beauty and Another [1998] 2 All ER 705.

Target Holdings Ltd v Redferns (a firm) [1995] 3 All ER 785, [1996] AC 421 at 434.

Tax Information Bulletin, Volume 6, No. 7, December 1994, New Zealand Inland Revenue Department.

Tax Information Bulletin, Volume 7, No. 8, February 1996, New Zealand Inland Revenue Department.

White v Vandervell Trustees and Inland Revenue Comrs [1971] AC 912 (House of Lords).

Acts of Parliament

The full text of the Australian Acts can be obtained on the Internet at www.rossholmes.co.nz/eptt_Australia.html#Legislation

The full text of the New Zealand Acts can be obtained on the Internet at www.rossholmes.co.nz/eptt_newzealand. html# Legislation or at public libraries.

Conveyancing Act 1919 (New South Wales, Australia).

Estate and Gift Duties Act 1968 (New Zealand).

Income Tax Act 1994 (New Zealand).

Land Transfer Act 1952 (New Zealand).

Minors (Property and Contracts) Act 1970 (New South Wales, Australia).

Property Law Act 1952 (New Zealand).

Real Property Act (Australia).

Social Security Act 1964 (New Zealand).

Ross Holmes is Managing Partner of Ross Holmes Lawyers (a law firm specialising in commercial and property law), Managing Director of Ross Holmes Limited (a company specialising in business, asset protection, trust and taxation planning), a director of a number of private companies and a trustee of the family trusts established by his family. Ross graduated with an honours degree in law from Victoria University (Wellington) in 1971. His degree included a masters paper in taxation and estate planning. He has been practising as a lawyer since 1973 and has been a partner in law firms since 1975.

Ross specialises in asset protection planning and trusts. He is an associate member of the prestigious international Society of Trust and Estate Practitioners (STEP). He has written several publications, including *Protect your Assets* (1996), its revised edition *Trusts* (1997), and *Sham Trusts* (1999), and is a contributing author to *Law of Trusts* (Butterworths). His experience in the asset protection planning field includes a period as senior manager in the taxation division of a leading accountancy firm, and a period as managing director of a trustee company subsidiary for the Australian and New Zealand Banking Group Limited. Ross gives regular seminars on trusts, entitled 'Success with Trusts' and 'Sham Trusts'.

Ross Holmes Limited has one of the largest asset protection planning teams in New Zealand. It operates in Auckland, Christchurch, Hamilton, Rotorua, Taupo, Tauranga, Taupo and Wellington.

New Zealand contact details:

P. O. Box 33-009
Albany
North Shore City
New Zealand

Telephone: 0800 TRUSTNZ or (64) (09) 415 0099

Fax: (64) (09) 415 0098

Email: rossholmes@rossholmes.co.nz

Website: www.estateplanning-trusts.com

Ross Holmes' other books on trusts include the following:

Asset Protection Planning, Trusts and the Administration of Trusts
This book is for those who have decided to form a trust, and those with a valid trust who need to know how to ensure that it succeeds and is run properly.

Sham Trusts
A guide for those with existing trusts. Learn why the majority of trusts are invalid. Learn how to avoid such unnecessary mistakes. This book contains what trustees need to know to make and record valid decisions.

To assist you achieve your objectives and prosper, visit the Ross Holmes Group's website at: www.estateplanning-trusts.com

> This website provides information on the following:
> — updates for this book,
> — worldwide asset protection planning and trust information,
> — asset protection planning and trust news,
> — a business planning guide,
> — a property guide,
> — an investment planning guide.